Contents

Introduction

The DATA reading scheme has been written to enable retarded and reluctant readers to master the skills of reading and to provide them with the experience in reading which is essential if they are to take their full part in our schools and our society.

This book has been written to help teachers to understand the approaches to the needs of these children implicit in the DATA scheme and to indicate ways in which teachers may help children acquire the skills of reading. It is written in the conviction that teaching a child to read in such a way that he will want to go on reading is one of the most vital and rewarding experiences a teacher may be privileged to enjoy.

DATA is the acronym formed from the words *D*evelopmental *A*pproach *T*eaching *A*id. The books and Workbooks of the scheme are aids: they will not teach the children to read. It is the rôle and function of the teacher to teach the child to read. The developmental approach to the child, to language development, to learning and to reading outlined in this book are guide-lines for success with the individual child who associates reading with failure. If they are applied with insight into the needs of the child and with the art and skill of the teacher then, instead of 'teaching reading', we may 'let the children read'.

Teaching reading has become a compulsive activity in our schools, progressively trivialised and barely understood. Large numbers of children still enter our junior and middle schools unable to read, whilst far too many children leave our schools semi-literate and certainly incapable of reading a novel. Many capable readers have been so badly taught that, in the words of David Holbrook, they are 'bookworms who will later bore only through pulp'. Teachers have been diverted from a concern for children and for our culture into a preoccupation with print. It is time the tide turned and we concentrated our attention upon the changing needs of the child.

The older child who regards reading as a threatening exposure of his vulnerability and incompetence or whose cultural deprivation is such that reading seems an alien activity, needs help quite outside the context of a 'remedial reading group' to which he may be assigned for half-an-hour a day. Certainly this is better than nothing, but teachers of such groups know how hard-won is their success when they can rarely go far enough back to the child's real need nor take him far enough forward to the stage where he has developed a lasting love of reading.

In the dead hearts of many of our cities, in the concrete deserts of estates and in caves twenty storeys high, generations of children are growing up for whom reading must be given a new and deeper significance than they will ever discern in the reading primers through which their fingers probe.

But, in our concern for the individual child, there is the danger that we see only the label on the file, the glib jargon that seems to say everything and says nothing: 'cross-lateral', 'developmental dyslexic', 'emotional block'. We should not see children as 'a challenge' or 'a problem' or as 'an interesting case of ideational agraphia' but see them as people, with all their strengths and needs, and welcome their presence in the infinite variety of human nature. We could not do better than Gerard Manley Hopkins and glory in

> All things counter, original, spare, strange;
> Whatever is fickle, freckled (who knows how?)
> With swift, slow; sweet, sour; adazzle, dim;[1]

[1] *Gerard Manley Hopkins 'Poems', Oxford University Press; from 'Pied Beauty'.*

If we can see both the 'outscape' of our world and the 'inscape' of the child's growing identity we may be able to see the child behind the retarded or reluctant reader and help that child to realise himself in the enjoyment and development of all that he can do.

We know what the child can't do. Our aim should be to see how he can excel in doing what he can do.

1 Success for Retarded Readers

'The funnel not the pump'

The first and essential aim in teaching retarded readers must be to give them success. It is not enough to diagnose difficulties: we must seek sources of success. It is not enough to know what a child can't do, we must find out what he can do and help him to excel in it. The dynamic base of the developmental approach to education is the striving of the growing child to succeed in his environment. The function of the teacher is to harness these drives to real and realisable goals.

Girls and boys in our society aged eight and over who are retarded in reading are deeply conscious of their failure and inadequacy. Every confrontation with print reinforces this sense of failure. Yet, too often, we persist in our efforts to help these children by seeking a new set of primers or we become hypnotised by diacritic marks, colour-coding or synthetic alphabets and ignore the evidence of the child's face. Confronting the poor reader with a page of print is like rubbing a puppy's nose in his dirt. The only difference is that we may cure the puppy but start the child soiling. We may succeed in teaching the child to read and imprint upon his mind the determination never to voluntarily open a book again in his life: our retarded reader has become a reluctant reader.

Successful teachers of reading don't teach reading: they create the conditions in which the child's desire to read coincides with his ability to read. This is the art and skill of teaching. In the words of Martin Buber, the teacher is 'the funnel not the pump'. We do not teach children to speak or to walk. Children start talking or trying to walk and we help them along. We provide encouragement, the most favourable conditions and our rewarding delight. Success builds upon success.

The advantaged reader

For the advantaged child learning to read progresses in exactly the same way. Secure in lap or bed, the child is rocked in the loom of language and song, rhyme and story. Soon, in the same conditions associated with pleasure and a growing mastery of language, he is being read to, being imprinted with print. Pictures are 'read' and talked about, prodded and peered into and then words are picked out and recognised, too. The secret is unwound from the print coiled along the lines of the page and, little by little, in spurts and starts, the code is decoded. From two onwards, words and letters begin to stand out both from the babble of language and the jumble of shapes. Words are sounds standing for things; print is encoded sound standing for words standing for things. And if, in this process of mastering a new skill, there are difficulties, mistakes, false starts and new barriers, all that matters is that the child can pick himself up again and know success.

Retrieval and self-realisation

When one considers the complexity of the process of reading the miracle is that so many children learn to read with such scant help. Advantaged children come to school at three or five able to read simple books and a little skilled teaching even makes them competent in the vagaries of our orthography. Interestingly enough, however, unless there is some skilled teaching many of these children will become avid readers whilst remaining poor spellers. There is no denying that reading is an acquired skill which, even for the most able and advantaged child, is not natural like breathing, walking or talking. The majority of retarded readers are retarded because they have not been adequately and appropriately helped to read.

The older retarded reader is a deprived child. The child who is socially, physically, culturally, emotionally or intellectually deprived and cannot read is doubly deprived. Whether we like it or not, the child born into our 'electronic global village' is born into a culture rooted in wood-pulp irrigated by printers' ink. The book is still the most efficient, economic and handiest machine for storing information, ideas and the verbalisation of our feelings and emotions. Reading is still the readiest means of retrieval. If we are to put the retarded reader back into the mainstream of our culture we have to find the resources within the child which will first remove the sense of failure and inadequacy and then use those strengths to train in the skills in which he is deficient. In the vast majority of cases success will be found by forgetting all about reading and taking a good, hard look at the child. Giving the advantage back to the disadvantaged child means helping the child to realise himself.

Instruction and the forceful search to develop

Pestalozzi, in 'How Gertrude Teaches her Children', written in 1801, describes the developmental approach precisely:

All human instruction is no more than the art of helping nature in its forceful search to develop in its own way, and this art depends primarily on the relation and harmony between the impressions to be made upon the child and the specific stage which his developing powers have reached at the time.

If we apply this approach to our retarded readers we see at once that 'the relation and harmony' between the child and print are making the wrong impressions. Our task must therefore be to restore equilibrium by 'helping nature in its forceful search to develop in its own way'.

Let's look at an actual example. Mike was ten and still couldn't read. Remedial efforts had given him the ability to bark at print, providing the print was limited to the simplest primers. His Reading Age was 6 years 9 months. A happy, physically robust boy he was well-adjusted to school and to his own poor academic performance. His teachers assumed that home was culturally deprived and linguistically deficient. Expectancy and arousal were clearly providing no motivation for academic success. Mike's report read: 'A pleasant, well-behaved lad who shows no interest in school work'. Staffroom

11

summation: 'A hewer of wood and a drawer of water'. Mother, on a rare visit to school: 'He's just like his dad'.

One Sunday afternoon, Mike was seen by his Head thirty miles from home, cycling along with a fishing-rod strapped to his crossbar. The Head suddenly saw a new dimension of Mike. He waylaid the boy on Monday morning and asked him about his fishing. Mike tried to explain. He chose simple words and phrases at first, unsure of the Head's ability to cope with the technicalities. The Head made encouraging noises. He didn't know a blacklure from a polystickle. He was out of his depth and tried a new approach. 'But how do you find your way, Mike?' Came the answer: 'Ordnance Survey maps, Sir. I mark them up. Of course it depends on the weather and the season and whether I'm going coarse fishing or for trout, Sir'. 'And you go on your own?' 'Mostly. The other kids aren't keen enough. You've got to be keen, Sir.' 'And what makes you so keen, Mike?' asked the Head. 'Well it was me Dad, Sir. He taught me when I was little but mostly it's the quiet, Sir, and sort of studying the rivers and the fish.' It reminded the Head of Izaak Walton's words, 'I love any discourse of rivers, and fish and fishing.'

Mike wasn't taught to read any more. He was invited to talk to his class about fishing. He took it very seriously and gave a model of what communication should be. He brought his tackle along, dressed himself up in his waders, passed round lures, demonstrated the art of casting and pin-pointed some, but by no means the most favoured, of the rivers he fished.

Thereafter, Mike learned to read by writing about fishing and by organising a club which was attended as enthusiastically by the Head and some of the staff as by the boys. He left junior school for his secondary education with a Reading Age of 12 years 5 months. At university he still found time to fish.

By accident, Mike was rescued just in time. Class 4S in a notorious secondary school are less fortunate. None of them can read but their teacher is trying to help them and give them some cultural enrichment at the same time. They are reading Joseph Conrad's 'The Nigger of the "Narcissus"' round the class, or that is the intention. The teacher recovers each weekend by going fishing. The boys 'recover' by wrecking their neighbourhood. Unless the art of teaching is applied, nature's 'forceful search to develop in its own way' will find other realisable and less desirable goals.

Unfulfilled needs for language

The identification of the areas in which we may give children success cannot be left to chance. They may be revealed systematically by careful observation and insight across the whole spectrum of development of the child in his physical, intellectual, emotional, cultural and social growth. At different times different needs will be uppermost. At different stages, in the egocentricity of infancy, in the biological explosion of adolescence, for instance, the interaction of the individual and his environment are most marked. But children are growing and changing all the time and their unfulfilled needs are forever pressing or else lying dormant to be reactivated. To argue that it is too late at eight (years or months) is to ignore the whole history of human development. Of course there are optimal periods of need which, if those needs are unfulfilled, may modify future growth but, just as we can today, to a very large extent, compensate for early malnutrition, so we may compensate for intellectual and cultural deprivation.

A classic example, of a late developer responding to the art of human instruction is that of Helen Keller and her teacher, Miss Sullivan, who communicated with her by touch. Helen Keller, it will be recalled, was blind, deaf and dumb. At the age of nearly seven she was over-ready to discover the secret of language. Yet, trapped as she was within the prison of an un-seeing, un-hearing and inarticulate body, it was not too late. She describes how she discovered language:

As the cool stream gushed over one hand she spelled into the other the word *water*, first slowly, then rapidly. I stood still, my whole attention fixed upon the motions of her fingers. Suddenly I felt a misty consciousness as of something forgotten—a thrill of returning thought; and somehow the mystery of language was revealed to me. I knew then that 'w-a-t-e-r' meant the wonderful cool something that was flowing over my hand. That living word awakened my soul, gave it light, joy, set it free! . . . . Everything had a name, and each name gave birth to a new thought.[1]

[1] *'The Story of my Life'* by Helen Keller, Hodder & Stoughton, London, 1959 ed.

Miss Sullivan, her teacher, had established communication with Helen Keller through the sense of touch and, by harmonising the impressions to be made upon her with her need to find the secret of language and the ability to think about the unseen and unheard world about her, had given her success and set her free.

This illustration of a handicapped child's discovery of language is particularly apposite to our concern for a developmental approach to the needs of retarded readers. We cannot here consider all the multitudinous factors operating upon the development of children, although any one factor may create an imbalance in a particular child's disposition to successful development. But we can narrow our concern to those areas particularly significant to the acquisition of the skill of reading.

The need for theories of knowledge and instruction

Although we may not wholly accept Jerome Bruner's assertion 'that any subject can be taught effectively in some intellectually honest form to any child at any stage' it should certainly challenge us to attempt to do so when the needs of the child demand it. Certainly we should accept his view that 'a theory of development must be linked both to a theory of knowledge and to a theory of instruction, or be doomed to triviality'.

If then, we are concerned with the individual child we must also be concerned with the nature of the knowledge which we wish him to gain and with the ways in which we may instruct him. Here, too, our approach is developmental. For reading itself is but a part of language which develops in the child in answer to the demands of the process of socialisation. Piaget begins his study of 'Language and Thought of the Child' by asking: 'What are the needs which a child tends to satisfy when he talks?' Unless we are to be doomed to triviality we must consider the retarded reader in the context of his language development. Here we will find the sources of success.

2 Reading and Language Development

Reading before print

Reading is the ability to gain and understand information from perceived stimuli. This basic animal behaviour is present and highly developed in all children in our schools, including those children who are deaf and blind. If a child is a non-reader of print he can still be given success in this basic form of reading and, the chances are, the exercise of this ability in association with language will establish in the child's mind the realisation that he can, in fact, read very successfully. An allegedly 'dyslexic' child the writer once met was certainly entirely competent in this activity and only began to make progress with print after he had been assured that he could already read.

The sky, the landscape, the tracks and droppings of animals were man's first texts. Shutting children up in schools and limiting their perception to print and lateral scanning is an invention of the Industrial Revolution which is only slowly, though recently quite rapidly in our primary schools, accommodating to the needs and nature of childhood and the realities of our world. It is only when we get children's heads out of their books that we begin to appreciate how little they know of the world around them. Frequently, when teachers do realise the extent of children's ignorance of the observable universe surrounding them, they send them scurrying back to their books to find out!

To gain and understand information from perceived stimuli we need to know much more than what we perceive at the time. The young child, for instance, will not recognise his own father (or mother) from a long way off simply because he does not know that, at a distance, objects appear smaller than they are. Later, the same child will have learned from experience to recognise his father from a long way off by a characteristic gesture imperceptible to anyone who did not know him well. The history of art demonstrates how recent is our understanding of perspective; optical illusions demonstrate how the mind mediates what is perceived.

The centrality of language

If we ask children to talk about what they perceive through their senses, we see another dimension of their problem. They can only talk about things they can name. In the infant classroom with the table, door and window inevitably labelled how many will refer to the architrave, hinges, the panes of glass or the thermoplastic tiling? On their 'nature walk' how many will know the names of the trees, plants, birds or physical features they see? Is the 'grass' lawn, meadow, field, spring-wheat, parkland or marsh? Not only is previous experience necessary but perception has to become progressively more discriminating, whilst understanding what is perceived entails the knowledge of words.

Yet 'naming the parts' is not language, any more than language is mere communication. Temporal and causal relationships, the 'before' and 'after', the 'Why?' and 'because', the shifts of meaning with context, are all part of our linguistic equipment. We use language for communicating information and for formulating our own thoughts. As Alice asked, 'How can I know what I think till I see what I say?' or, on the other hand, as the little boy pondered, 'I see what I mean but I don't know how to say it'. We use language as gesture, as an escapement for our over-wound feelings and as social grooming. From the reading of signs which signify in our perceptual field we proceed to the signs by which socialised man signals his thoughts crystalised in language.

Language and socialisation

It is tempting, then, to say 'Let the children talk' and to fondly imagine that children talking together about what they are doing will generate their own language development. Once teachers seemed to believe that, placed in experiential situations (the sand-pit or paddling-pool), children would in fact, through being involved together in 'purposeful play', develop their language abilities. Nothing could be further from the truth. Without the intervention of adults or of children with higher levels of language development there can be very little progress in the use or understanding of language. Left to themselves they may well be reinforcing structures and inadequate vocabulary they might otherwise have outgrown. As language is the result of socialisation it is only from society that a child may gain language. The richer the social and cultural environment of the child, the richer its language, the more advanced its thinking. If the home has not provided the child with a rich vocabulary and an elaborate code of linguistic structures, then the school must provide them.

For many retarded readers, especially those from culturally impoverished backgrounds, their primary need is not the ability to read but the ability to talk and to think. The advantaged child comes to school at five with a large vocabulary and familiarity with virtually all the structures of language. Moreover, he will be able to shift from one appropriate register of language to another with ease, turning from a conversation with an adult to what Dylan Thomas called 'the tumble and rhyme' of language which children use with one another.

The culturally disadvantaged child of five will have a limited vocabulary and be more familiar with the imperative (Shut up! Get out! Come 'ere!) than the teacher's subjunctive 'If I were you . . . .' Unless the school can provide compensatory education which enables deprived children to enrich their language there is little value in teaching them to read, for the language development of children is the intellectual development of children and children with limited language ability are children with limited intellectual ability.

Language and retarded readers

What can we do about the language development of the older retarded reader who is inarticulate and retarded in language development? It could be argued that by teaching him to read we will give him the ability to enrich his vocabulary and knowledge of structures. In some instances and to some extent this may be true. But if the child

17

is already finding difficulty in reading it is unlikely to prove the successful course to pursue. If we put ourselves in the child's place we can see his problem. We can read already so it will not take us long to learn Cyrillic script and learn to read Russian which is, like i.t.a., phonetically consistent. With a little practice we can now read 'War and Peace' aloud to our admiring friends—and not understand a word of it! There are many children in our schools doing just that. But, unfortunately for them, with even less success for they have to struggle with our orthography. What little meaning they are able to dredge up from the page leads only to 'confusion worse confounded'.

Only directed, strongly motivated, purposeful experience in a language-rich situation can meet the needs of these children. The approach to science in primary schools of the Nuffield Project[1] was an outstanding example of what is needed. We must find what provokes the curiosity and triggers off the exploratory drives of the children and let them explore and find answers to their own questions while we help them with the words and the structures the situations demand. We must read and talk and discuss and question and probe with them—and read to them. Their own questions will highlight their needs, our questions will change their perspectives upon the situations. Our replies to their questions should not be closures but open up for them new lines of enquiry, new relationships, new attitudes, and help to provide some of the words and structures they need. Our conversation about significant experience enjoyed by the child will change his consciousness of the experience and develop his thinking about it only if our language extends and elaborates the child's limited verbalisation.

Rich experience has to involve the whole child over the whole perceptual range—through hearing, touch, sight, smell and taste—and be heightened and made conscious by language. If the intellect of the child is to be involved then there must be an absence of stress and tension, for the greater the stress the lower the level of intellectual functioning. We can barrack and bawl our way into children's consciousness and jerk their strings like electronic puppets, and maybe in 'ratomorphic' psychology this will pass as SR learning, but

[1] *'Nuffield Junior Science, Teacher's Guides 1 & 2', Collins, London, 1967.*

no matter how efficient this approach may prove to be in teaching skills it will never enable the child to learn to learn.

The extension of language will require a heightening of auditory perception and discrimination. In the simplest terms, in the most potent situation, this means rapt attention to the teller of tales. Language is magic and the child from the culturally deprived background knows little of it. He was 'cabined, cribbed, confined, bound in' his crêche when he should have been lap-learning the warp and weft and wonder of language on his mother's knee. The fun and fantasy, the fabulous of the ordinary, rhyme, myth and legend have been missing but can now reawaken his senses and his mind to wonder. Only in this way will new words awaken new consciousness and old words become enlarged in their reverberations within him; expectantly listening, he must feel the words weaving their magic through his senses. If we can achieve this we have replicated the good mum's lap he lacked.

The opportunities and incentives we give to the child to talk about the experience he has enjoyed will increase his conscious choice of words and structures and he will progress from 'I do and I understand' to 'I say, I know and I have made my own'. Changing the situation from casual conversation to one requiring explanation, the determination of causality, summation or inference will extend the structures used. It will also demand new rhythms, cadences and inflexions in speech and require conscious concern for clarity of articulation and precision of thought. All this will bring new confidence and new power. For language gives us power over our environment as well as over ourselves. And what the socially deprived child lacks is a positive posture towards his environment: his environment acts upon him and, in defence, he already adopts a fatalistic or hostile attitude towards it.

Language and social posture

Much more important than the difference between the elaborated formal code of language used by the advantaged child and the restricted, public code of the socially disadvantaged which Bernstein has so clearly delineated, is the difference of posture each adopts towards his society and environment. There is a gulf between, say, the son of the tycoon who negotiates a successful take-over bid and the son of the unskilled worker who loses his job as an indirect result. One father hangs an original Lowry on his wall and takes the family out to dinner to celebrate, whilst the other hopes his football pools will 'come up' and doesn't know how to claim the benefits to which he is entitled. Each child feels the effects in the cognitive and affective domains as well as in his belly, of course.

How important it is, therefore, that the child from a socially or culturally deprived background should gain self-awareness and confidence in school. Can we hope to give it to him in school? It is surprising the extent to which the good school can succeed in determining realisable goals. The A.A.A. 5 Star Award scheme is an excellent example of encouraging children to improve their physical prowess without the disadvantages of unequal competition. The school which spawns a chess club, band, amateur radio station, grows crops, cares for the handicapped and aged, keeps fish and animals, produces pots, poetry, 'pop' and plays is a far, far better place than the examination factory which performs a ritual murder of Shakespeare's set play as its sacrifice to Culture. In the good, lively school the retarded and reluctant readers will not be consigned to the dimmest, youngest, least experienced teacher in the annexe but will be learning to live and to grow in stature and confidence with the most versatile, youngest-in-mind-and-richest-in-experience teacher and fully involved in all the vital and significant activities of the school. Thus will they enrich their language, learn to think and learn to learn.

Language and recording

Only with enriched language derived from rich experience can children begin to approach reading print successfully. To see the full significance of this let us look again at man's development anthropologically.

Primitive man, as we have seen, read the evidence of his universe and gained mastery over it, and himself, through his developing consciousness. In this process language played a key role. Only later did the need to record arise although he will early have displayed his ability to leave his mark upon his territory. From making his mark by blazing his trail on trees to notching a stick to count his cattle or wives is a short step, although we know it took an unconscionable long time. How long it took him to progress from sign to symbol, from symbol to pictogram and from pictogram to ideogram or logogram spans the history of mankind. But all of these methods of recording preserve and present something of the sense of what they represent whether pictorially, symbolically or ideationally.

Children retrace these steps when they finger-paint in their stewed prunes, draw trees like lollipops or make block-charts and histograms. It is essential that we understand what is involved in these processes ourselves and create the situations in which children can develop the appropriate understanding and skill. Many retarded readers need help in recording and in reading signs and symbols seen in everyday life (e.g. ×, !, +, —, etc.). The need to record and the ability to record pre-dates developmentally the ability to read. The child who has recorded what he has done in any form will have little difficulty in talking about what he has recorded. In mathematics we also encourage him to go beyond the stage of retelling what has been recorded and foster the development of the abilities to quantify, to categorise, to establish relationships, to interpret and to infer from what has been recorded.

This ability to read what has been recorded by the child himself, and then by other children, establishes both the encoding and decoding process. The infant paints her picture and the wise teacher asks her to tell her about it. She doesn't baldly ask, 'What is it supposed to be?' because she knows that, for the child, it is what the child determined it to be. Equally important, the child is becoming familiar, at a level of relevance appropriate to his own development in concrete situations, with the snags and snares of the encoding-decoding process. For gradually, as the child matures, egocentric symbolisation fails to satisfy the demands for more logical, and precise representation. Experience in art and in crafts, in mathematics, drama, music and science, all contribute to the development of concepts and classifications of sets, sub-sets and of relationships.

The child knows that the representation of the thing is not the thing itself and that the idea of the thing is abstracted into the sign or symbol. Now the model or the crosses on a chart which stand for things can be manipulated independently: 'The chart shows that John is taller than Mary, and Mary and John are shorter than David'. What began as magic becomes mathematically logical. Without this development the reading of what has been recorded is impossible.

The reading of print involves another leap forward which we must examine more closely. Before we do so, let us return to our retarded child. If he cannot read, has he the language and the ability to think which will make reading meaningful? If not, we must enrich his vocabulary, enlarge his use of structures and increase his familiarity with the registers of language whether they be of home, street, books or of his teachers. We can do this by involving him in directed, purposeful experience in which his perceptual and language development is deliberately fostered in a stress-free, stimulating and expectant atmosphere in which he can be successful. Arising from this experience we can generate the need to record in a variety of ways appropriate to both the child and the situations. At the same time we can foster the child's self-awareness and self-confidence and develop in him a positive posture to his environment so that he both reacts to it and acts upon it effectively. We can enrich his experience of language by reading to him, by telling him tales, jingles, rhymes and poems, by letting him listen to recordings of verse and plays, and so awaken his feelings and senses to the magic and the power of language and the wonder of his universe.

And if we do none of these things, either because we cannot or think we need not, then we owe the retarded or reluctant reader at least one small but vital consideration. We must not insult him by expecting him to read words he does not understand in structures with which he is unfamiliar about situations outside his experience or imagining. If you think you can short-cut the teaching of reading by ignoring the child's need for language then try this: Strč prst skrz krk!

3 *Reading Print*

Print in perspective

Reading print needs putting in perspective. There is no doubt about its importance in our culture and, therefore, to our children. But it certainly is not a natural human activity like breathing or talking and mass literacy is both a recent and a threatened phenomenon. Just how recent mass literacy is, is shown by the facts that, in the census of 1851, of 30 000 private schoolteachers 700 could not write their own names, and that, only a century ago, over a quarter of the adult population of England and Wales was completely illiterate. We are getting things quite out of perspective if we generate over-anxiety about literacy and spelling or are ourselves so imprinted with print that we think the ability to read 'those damned little black marks' has anything whatsoever to do with intelligence. Yet it is only a few decades since 'intelligence tests' equated innate intelligence with the ability to respond to print with print. Again, it is not without significance that some of the greatest advances in intellectual development in mathematics, science, technology and the arts have been made possible through man's ability to think without words. This is not to dispute the centrality of language but merely to establish that there is more to life and our ability to think about it than trivia such as infants' reading ability assessed according to 'primer criterion' having predictive value for future academic success. To state that in our print culture the early ability to read print indicates academic potential is a statement of the obvious.

A cybernetic model of development

The arguments about nature and nurture in the context of socio-economic factors affecting children's academic success can be resolved quite simply and logically by recognising that, in cybernetic terms, there is no dichotomy between nature and nurture but simply feedback. Piaget explains it with brilliant insight:

> In the development of the child, there is no pre-established plan, but a gradual evolution in which each innovation is dependent upon the previous one. Adult thought might seem to provide a pre-established model, but the child does not understand adult thought until he has reconstructed it, and thought is itself the result of an evolution carried on by several generations, each of which has gone through childhood. Any explanation of the child's development must take into consideration two dimensions: an ontogenetic dimension and a social dimension (in the sense of the transmission of the successive work of generations). However, the problem is somewhat analogous in both cases, for in both the central question concerns the internal mechanism of all constructivism.
>
> An internal mechanism (though it cannot be reduced to heredity alone and has no pre-established plan, since there is in fact construction) is observable at the time of each partial construction and each transition from one stage to the next. It is a process of equilibrium, not in the sense of a simple balance of forces, as in mechanics, or an increase of entropy, as in thermodynamics, but in the sense—which has now been brought out so clearly by cybernetics—of self-regulation; that is, a series of active compensations on the part of the subject in response to external disturbances and an adjustment that is both retroactive (loop systems or feedbacks) and anticipatory, constituting a permanent system of compensations.[1]

If we see children's development in our print culture as a continuous process of self-regulation in which the growing, changing child seeks coherence and equilibrium between all the complex interactions of its need to grow, to assert itself, to succeed, to love and be loved, to respond to the drive of curiosity, and the stimuli of its total social context, then we must recognise that our own adult 'pre-established model' of thought about our culture and our method of instruction should relate both to the child and to the child's reality. This we are still largely failing to do because our own thinking is too deeply rooted in wood-pulp.

[1] *'The Psychology of the Child'* by *J. Piaget and Bärbel Inhelder, Routledge & Kegan Paul Ltd., London, 1969.*

The impingement of TV's mosaic image

We may appear to be a long way from the pressing needs of reluctant readers but it is essential that we look at reality with objectivity. This is what Marshall McLuhan perceived of the reality in which our children live today:

> The young people who have experienced a decade of TV have naturally imbibed an urge toward involvement in depth that makes all the remote, visualized goals of usual culture seem not only unreal but irrelevant, and not only irrelevant but anaemic. It is the total involvement in all-inclusive *nowness* that occurs in young lives via TV's mosaic image . . . It is, of course, our job not only to understand this change, but to exploit its pedagogical richness. The TV child expects involvement and doesn't want a specialist *job* in the future. He does want a *rôle* and a deep commitment to his society.[1]

The fact is that our print culture has already been changed and, with the greater impact of colour TV, will soon change even more dramatically. What are some of the obvious changes?

Instead of queues on the quays of New York for the latest instalment of Dickens, streets, churches, clubs are emptied by a TV presentation of Dickens. The family Bible reading, the family visit to church or chapel are activities of the past and the TV flickers in every living-room. Newspapers no longer compete with being first with the news: it was 'seen' the night before and the papers have become daily magazines, the magazines having largely perished. Libraries, in competition at first with TV, now service it, providing the information books to satisfy the interests sparked off by TV together with copies of the novels being serialised. Children see and hear in a minute on TV more information than they could hope to acquire from an hour's reading. The impact of events on the other side of the planet or the Moon is immediate and immediately comprehensible to us. Because the impact is immediate, and not mediated through print, action is almost simultaneous and happenings in Berkeley, California, are copied in Tokyo or London as rôle-seeking adolescents realise new rôles to play.

---

[1] *'Understanding Media: the Extensions of Man'* by Marshall McLuhan, Routledge & Kegan Paul Ltd., London, 1964.

We not only need to harmonise our messages to the needs of the child but also to harmonise them with the other messages the child is perceiving. If we are to encourage children to read print, as indeed we should, we must understand the differences between reading print and reading our physical landscape, and also understand the changes in our culture.

Reading and meaning

Reading print is the activity of retrieving language encoded in alphabetic symbols by lateral scanning from left to right so that, when decoded into sounds which are synthesised into words, the words in their context, have meaning. This is a complex but still inadequate definition of an activity we take too much for granted, perhaps, but one which we need to understand in all its complexity if we are to help retarded children. Unless you knew Czech, for example, you could not read 'Strč prst skrz krk!'[1] because, no matter how successful you were in recombining the sounds of the phonetically consistent alphabet, there was no meaning.

The child who reads 'The albatross was perched on the bowsprit' or 'The owl flew to the farm and landed on the barn' or 'To be or not to be' has to contend with a variety of problems quite distinct from those connected with the problem of lateral scanning or combining sounds into words. The first sentence cannot be illustrated to clarify meaning unless the child understands at least one of the words of more than three letters; some children who could cope with 'flew' and 'landed' in the second sentence might deduce 'owl' as being a bird but would not understand 'barn'—one explanation a teacher received from a child of seven was 'a big building with a cross on top'. And the easiest sentence to read (R.A. 4.5?) is the hardest to understand and not even a dictionary will help us. Yet seven-year-olds who could not cope with the print could understand all three sentences in the context of TV.

[1] *A sentence of Czech consonants meaning 'Stick your finger through your neck!' and thus popular with children.* (č = ch).

26

We have already emphasised the importance of the child's language and thought being developed to a sufficiently adequate level to make reading a meaningful activity and it is self-evident that children must understand what they read before they have read it. The reading of print is the retrieval of language. But unlike speech, which is sound arranged in time, reading is the decoding of symbols for sounds arranged laterally. Unfortunately, we too often overestimate children's language endowment and do not recognise the confusion wrought in their minds as word succeeds word without clarity of meaning. Because the child must scan laterally, letters and sometimes whole words and phrases must be held in the memory until they have been resolved and 'cleared' by the total context. For example, if we read 'The bat was in the bag . . .' we are perfectly clear what each word means, unless, of course, we read on to find that the next words say '. . . and was fast asleep'. The reverse situation obtains when one word cues us to expect a string of words as, for example, when we read 'Once upon . . .' we anticipate 'a time there was'. In English, with its many homonyms, the spelling is also a cue. 'Here . . .' and 'Hear . . . !' elicit quite different expectations. Children who have learned to read with a phonetically consistent alphabet have been denied these clues to meaning and structure. Reduced to phonetic consistency 'meat' and 'meet' or 'where' and 'wear' may be marginally easier to read but are entirely dependent upon their context for their meaning. This does not cause confusion or uncertainty in speech because speed, stress, inflexion all contribute to clarity. If we are concerned with meaning then retarded readers need all the cues and clues our inconsistent orthography gives them.

Helping the retarded reader with meaning

We can help retarded readers by ensuring that they are thoroughly familiar with the vocabulary and the situations they are going to meet before they begin reading. We can help them still further by 'response reading'. If we read a sentence clearly and naturally and ask the child to read the same sentence aloud, whilst following with finger and eye the line of print, we ensure that print, sound, meaning, voice, hand and eye are in harmony. The child is confident of success and concentrates in particular upon co-ordination of hand and eye as he responds. He reads, speaks and understands what he sees before he says it. Brief spells of 'response reading' during which concentration, hand-eye co-ordination, clear articulation and meaningful inflexion are expected, restore confidence, encourage internalisation of reading and emphasise the importance of reading for meaning. The load on the child's weak decoding mechanism is borne by the teacher.

We can help the poor reader considerably, too, by talking about the illustrations of the text he is about to read and by taking care that we use the words and structures of the text. By our questions we can encourage the child to use the words and structures and, by encouraging the child to ask questions, determine how well he understands the situations he will meet.

The Rank Audio Visual 'Language Master' and E. J. Arnold's 'Ricoh Synchrofax Audio Page' machines, which reproduce the teacher's or child's voice from the card or sheet on which pictures, words or sentences have been printed, provide help to the child very similar to that given by 'response reading'. Many schools have produced programmes which proceed from pictures with words 'on sound', step by step, to sentences in print with sentences 'on sound'. These are followed by books in which the child meets the same sentences in solitary print. At every stage the teacher first teaches the child and uses the machine as a means to provide repetition and the involvement of the child who can record his own response and check it against the teacher's 'master' recording. The process is thus a series of self-regulating loops, the teacher controlling the input, both visually and aurally, and monitoring the feed-back from the child. They are the only tools available which are both flexible enough to provide individual programming and the input of both sound and print simultaneously. As with all tools in education, the success of such programmes depends entirely upon the child-teacher relationship and on the skill of the teacher in providing appropriate material. If these are assumed, then there is no doubt that for the first time in history we have tools which help the teacher to teach reading skills by reproducing her voice in association with print and enabling the child to record and monitor his own responses.

These are a few of the ways in which we can help the retarded reader but, before exploring other methods, we should ask ourselves whether or not it is possible to introduce reading in such a way that there can be no doubt whatsoever that the child knows and understands the text before he reads it.

The natural approach to reading and the solution to the problem of ensuring that the child understands the language he reads is common in infant schools and in the education of the physically handicapped. If, as has already been suggested, we encourage children to record in pictures, charts, symbols and diagrams, in two- and three-dimensions and to talk about what they have recorded, then the natural progression is to encourage them to record in writing. Infant teachers frequently write on children's pictures and encourage them to 'response-read' and to copy or trace what has been written. This introduction to the encoding and lateral, left-right, system removes all the uncertainties which beset both teacher and child dependent upon primers. Only known language, derived from known, significant situations, is being recorded and retrieved by the child and the kinaesthetic experience of writing reinforces the alphabetic encoding system.

This can be successfully extended to encouraging the child to make his own book, using his own pictures and those chosen and cut out by him. The need for titles and text will arise naturally and, quite apart from all the hand-eye dexterities deployed in these activities, will introduce the child, in a context in which he is strongly motivated, to pursue an individual interest and make something of the encoding-decoding of language.

The importance of care at the early stages of reading are more than ever important today when children are impatient with print's lack of immediacy. The methods suggested are also important because they establish the meaningful nature of recording in print. It cannot be too strongly stated that *the best book for a child to begin reading is the book he has made for himself.*

Perceptual problems of decoding print

The left-right alphabetic-phonic problem has received so much attention that there is little need for us to devote attention to the matter here. Prof. M. D. Vernon, after examining the evidence of the factors of a visual, auditory, cognitive, social and emotional nature associated with reading disability, writes:

> A multiple of factors are associated with reading backwardness in different cases, but there are no factors which appear in all cases. Or rather, the methods of experiment and clinical diagnosis so far employed have failed to isolate any factors which appear universally in all cases of reading backwardness—other than inability to read easily.[1]

Many of the perceptual difficulties of children can be diagnosed by such tests as Daniels and Diack's[2] whilst the 'Programmed Reading Kit' of D. H. Stott provides, in game-playing situations, exercise in letter recognition and blending so that, step by step, phonically graded vocabulary is established. The game-playing of the 'Programmed Reading Kit'[3] is particularly valuable with older retarded readers, for whom it was developed, and one of its most valuable functions is the growth in concentration span developed by the very-much-involved participants.

For readers concerned with children with severe perceptual dysfunction the work of Dr. Marianne Frostig is lucidly described in Mary Arkwright's 'The Frostig Approach'[4] whilst the most recent book surveying the whole field of reading disability is Emerald Dechant's 'Diagnosis and Remediation of Reading Disability'.[5] For the general teacher of reading Donald Moyle's 'The Teaching of Reading'[6] is essential reading.

[1] *'Backwardness in Reading'* by M. D. Vernon, Cambridge University Press, London, 1957.
[2] *'The Standard Reading Tests'* by J. C. Daniels & Hunter Diack, Chatto & Windus, London, 1958.
[3] *'The Programmed Reading Kit'*, D. H. Stott, W. & R. Holmes, 1962.
[4] *'The Frostig Approach'* by M. Arkwright, The College of Special Education, London, W.1., 1969.
[5] *'Diagnosis and Remediation of Reading Disability'* by E. Dechant, Parker Pub. Co. Inc., New York, 1968.
[6] *'The Teaching of Reading'* by D. Moyle, Ward Lock Educational, London, 1968.

But, in practice, the dedicated teachers of reading—and their work is insufficiently known or appreciated—rarely find that other people's methods work as effectively as their own. Over the years they have developed their own insights into children's difficulties and their own techniques, borrowing here, adding there. What is invariably significant is the stress they place, whether consciously or not, upon their relations with the children. This is by no means to underestimate the value of their techniques. It is essential for any teacher who wishes to emulate them, but who has not studied in depth the complexities of reading disabilities, to proceed from the following bases:

  (i) Establish relaxed confidence, predisposition to success and a sense of fun in the child;

 (ii) Determine what the child can do in language skills (speech, understanding and response to speech, encoding of language in signs, symbols or writing and their decoding) and retreat to a point at which the child is secure;

(iii) Develop activities at the point of confidence and certainty which gradually lead to encoding in writing by the child so that words and sentences spoken by the child are written and read by him; yesterday's texts become today's and tomorrow's code-book or dictionary;

 (iv) Don't make a frontal assault on difficulties and disabilities: use strengths to overcome deficiencies and treat defects of the locomotor, hand-eye co-ordinatory type outside the context of reading and writing (in art and craft, PE, drama, games);

  (v) Encourage attentive listening to sounds in speech and music, especially singing; make the child conscious of language and use a word in a variety of ways and contexts; get the child asking and answering questions;

 (vi) Establish directionality in writing-patterns, in writing and encoding and in reading;

(vii) Establish sound-word relationship and sound-letter-pattern relationship in meaningful contexts;

(viii) Maintain curiosity and exploratory drives of child at a high level by using fun, novelty and games and never hurry to the next step until the child's response is automatic;

31

(ix) Response-reading and listening, whilst following text with hand and eye as teacher reads, will encourage internalisation and automatisation of reading at all levels;

(x) Praise the child for his successes; if he hasn't any, then re-start at (i), (ii) or (iii) above.

Sound sense

The phonic aspect of print will always present difficulty. We cannot pronounce 'Read' without a context and we should not discourage guessing providing guesses are based on the letter clues and are appropriate *words*. One of the easiest ways of establishing the sound-sense principle is to encourage children to 'guess' the initial sound of a word and then show them the letter; this can be extended to the final sound and to the middle sound of words. Games of 'I Spy' and 'My Grandmother's Cat' further extend this consciousness of words and the sounds they contain. We must remember here that children may not know what 'sounds' and 'words' are until we have established their meaning and significance. Nor can we be sure that they recognise words as individual units. A two-year-old told by her mother, 'You mustn't argue, dear', replied, 'If you arg me, I'll arg you!' Many older readers may not be much further developed in their understanding of many words—as we know from their strange versions of hymns and prayers!

Onomatopoeic and echoic words are the only words which mean what they sound and which, usually, can be relied upon to be spelt phonetically. They provide us with a unique opportunity for involving the children in games in which they guess what the words mean when they hear or see them. From 'Oh!' and 'Ah!', 'Eh?' and 'Ugh!' we can proceed in gentle steps to 'hiss', 'flop', 'slither' and 'whisper'. At each stage we must establish the encoding principle and, having done so, encourage the children to respond with the sound when they see the letters. Soon the children will be inventing their own sounds and the echoic words for them and enjoying the 'slithy toves'. Words will give delight and provoke laughter—children who can laugh at words will learn to read.

To assist teachers in this vital stage of the skill a list of echoic and onomatopoeic words, by no means exhaustive but certainly exhausting, is given in Appendix A.

Nude words

But for some children there is another difficulty. They can make the sound of the word but, because they have seen the word in print, find difficulty in associating the word with its meaning. We can put ourselves in their position and discover once and for all that the word is not the thing by following the instructions of William James in his 'Principles of Psychology' published in 1890:

> If we look at an isolated printed word and repeat it long enough, it ends by assuming an entirely unnatural aspect . . . its body is indeed there, but its soul is fled. It is reduced, by this new way of attending to it, to its sensational nudity. We never before attended to it in this way, but habitually got it clad with its meaning the moment we caught sight of it, and rapidly passed from it to other words of the phrase. We apprehended it, in short, with a cloud of associates, and thus perceiving it, we felt it quite otherwise than as we feel it now, divested and alone.

Children who come to school with words still embedded in phrases, like the child who says 'Skoos?' for 'Please may I be excused?' will undoubtedly find difficulty in recognising words seen alone in their 'sensational nudity'. We can help them orally and improve auditory discrimination and we can also help them calligraphically and typographically.

In some of the early DATA books and workbooks we have de-

```
                                                c
                        s                       r
liberately introduced typograms such as  p    h  and cross  to assist
                        l s                     s
                        a                       s
```

children not merely to enjoy the fun of playing with words but also to awaken an awareness of 'the sensational nudity of words' and of their ideographic possibilities which are absent in our alphabetic print but present in Chinese logograms. Baroque poetry and, more recently, the calligrammes of Guillaume Apollinaire, Paul Klee's pictographs and ideograms give this form a thoroughly respectable pedigree, if one is needed, to release it from the maw of advertisements ('Sch . . .'). Children need to develop an awareness of words and the letters that compose them and this is but one way in which we may help them whilst giving them delight and exercising their imaginations. Through 'concrete poetry' and 'writing patterns' they may be helped to progress to verse and poetry. In the words of John Dewey: 'Children are people. They grow into tomorrow only as they live today'.

Sign reading and the arrow

The directionality of our printed language entails that children need to know their left from their right and many of them don't. Children who cannot read print understand an arrow without difficulty: it is man's most potent and universal symbol. It has been used in the first of the DATA books to establish for teacher and child the value of reading symbols and signs as a way of enjoying success in reading without print and also as a means of encouraging directional attack on print. Children who are cross-lateral or ambidexterous may (but not necessarily) need help and the arrow and other symbols have a compelling force which teachers can use to help them. However, developing hand-and-eye co-ordinatory skills in PE and games, in art and craft will also play an important part. But there is a danger that time may be wasted on them. If, instead, we look for strengths we may find far shorter routes to overcoming these difficulties. Thus, the highly verbal child may respond to a sympathetic explanation of what he is required to do, a child with slight high-frequency hearing loss may be helped by being encouraged to watch his teacher's lips. Because we have diagnosed difficulties we should not make a frontal assault on them but use the child's strengths to overcome them and bring into play motivation, self-awareness and well-established channels of communication.

But above all, we must determine from the beginning that what the child gains from the activity of reading is itself self-rewarding. We are competing with the *nowness* of the TV image and the immediacy of its sight-sound communication. Reading primers cannot compete with this and, although they may prove successful with infants who find their reward both in the mastery of a new skill and the delight of parents and teachers, the older retarded readers have already been rejected by them and have themselves rejected them.

The skill of reading print defined

Reading, like child development, may be seen in cybernetic terms: the input of the print is coded information which is decoded and the feed-back, which regulates the process, is our ability to maintain interest in the output, the meaning of the language. The process of reading must result in our gaining information and maintaining concentration. To be complete, any definition of reading must include this rewarding, self-regulating aspect of the process. Without exploring the intricacies of all that the process involves we would define reading in these terms:

Reading print is the automatised, self-rewarding, cultural activity of retrieving language encoded in alphabetic symbols by left to right lateral scanning so that, when decoded into sounds which are synthesised into words, the words in their context have meaning.

The rôle of illustrations is significant in this context. If the child receives more information from the illustrations than from the text, the value of reading has been diminished. Some children's books overload the circuit pictorially and, by making meaning immediately accessible, detract from the value of the text. A picture of roast beef and Yorkshire pudding with the words 'Look—food!' beneath it reduces reading to unrewarding pointlessness. The 'Dr. Seuss' books, on the other hand, use illustrations to evoke strong motivation to read the text which releases new information to enhance the significance of both picture and text.

However, it cannot be assumed that illustrations, because they are explicit to the adult and relate to the text, necessarily aid the child. If, for instance a child sees a simple picture of a child playing with a ball in a garden and reads 'The ball is on the . . .' he may anticipate from the picture 'grass', 'ground', 'garden' or none of these. The word could be 'lawn'. If his guess or attempt at synthesis is wrong, the next sentence containing the word may put him right or further confuse him. Children left to fend for themselves in this type of situation may regress and give up the unequal struggle. The Gestalt, whole-word, approach, and the pure sentence method, must be underpinned both with prior knowledge of the vocabulary and with a knowledge of the phonic code.

The child's understanding of illustrations

With culturally deprived, as with very young children, a few minutes talking about a picture may reveal surprising gaps in vocabulary. Three ten-year-old girls in an urban junior school described a picture of boats in a bay as 'country'; pressed for a word more appropriate to the scene, one suggested 'Scotland'. None knew 'port', 'mast', 'harbour', 'bay', flagpole'.

One of the easiest ways of determining children's vocabulary deficiencies is to ask them about the parts of the body. Despite the fact that they may 'do' PE every day many children of eight and over are remarkably unaware and find obscure such simple words as wrist, knuckle, joint, spine, eyelid, eyebrow, nostril, bridge and instep. A few games such as 'O'Grady Says', rather than object lessons, may soon put this right and will be found to increase their self-awareness and self-confidence. It is yet another example of the need to increase perception by progressively refining observation and discrimination. Activities such as these provide a ready and useful vocabulary to record, excite curiosity and lead to open-ended exploratory activities which will enrich language and thought. They will also indicate the need for caution in the assumptions we make about the children's ability to derive clues to vocabulary from illustrations.

The illustrations in children's books must be realistic, visually attractive, possess selective emphasis (which is sometimes difficult to achieve in photographs), promote understanding, stimulate the desire to read, complement and supplement the text and assist in the meaningful organisation of the information retrieved from the laterally organised print. The illustrations of the 'Zig and Zag' books meet these requirements and few adults reading the books have recognised that nowhere in the stories are Zig and Zag described, whilst their spaceship is only described in two or three words of the text. By the application of cybernetic principles of design[1] the impact of the text

[1] *See Chapter 5, The Design of Data, page 42.*

and the illustrations is of a completely integrated experience. It is in this way that we have attempted to reach out towards the child with the immediacy of impression to which TV has accustomed him.

The experience of living with television and with the signs and symbols of our streets is exploited in 'Told by an Arrow', the 'Zig and Zag' books, the 'cowboy' books and 'Once upon a space'. The reality of the children's own world provides the core of the 'Bruff' books and 'Fly away Paul', whilst the reality they perceive around them and their mediated experience through the mass-media are united in 'In Fact'. Thus we have attempted to place the books within the social context of the child today. It is hoped that an understanding by the teacher of the individual child and of the child's real world will enable the books and the child to be brought into harmony. But, we repeat, it cannot be assumed that pictures alone provide vocabulary no matter how much they may assist understanding.

4 *The Child's Regard for Himself*

Signature . . .

The first need we must satisfy is that of the child's need for an image of himself. We have stressed throughout the importance to the child of success, of self-awareness and self-confidence, and of growing consciousness of himself and the world around him. We can only contribute to the child's self-knowledge and growth if we know the child and his needs in depth. Our concern, care, affection, belief and interest, expressed in our face and the quality of our voice, are essential factors in our ability to help his development. But we need knowledge both of the child and of how to act.

One of the most pathetic stories the author has heard in connection with the rôle of literacy in our society is that of Maud, a 46-year-old woman who was completely illiterate. A colleague decided he would try to help her where, clearly, so many had failed. Instead of launching into elaborate diagnostic procedures and evolving a complex programme of remedial measures he did something profoundly simple. Having gained her confidence, he taught her to write her own name. The process took a total of three hours. The following day Maud went to the post-office and, for the first time in her life, signed her own name on a withdrawal form. The technique used to teach Maud to write her own name was precisely that used by infant teachers: tracing and copying. The effect upon Maud was little short of miraculous.

If, throughout their development, children are seeking to establish their image of themselves and their own identity, can our reluctant and retarded readers write their own names with accuracy and fluency? Their own names mean more to them than all the print in the dictionary. And can they write the names of their parents, family and friends, and the address of their home? If we will help them to do so–clearly, accurately and fluently–we will have enhanced their image of themselves and have taught them an enormous amount of the encoding system, together with some of the subtleties of spelling.

The Workbooks in the DATA scheme contain numerous opportunities for the children to write about themselves, their activities and interests,[1] and later about their views and opinions. Clearly these are things they will want to do and be able to do. But they are also provided for the teacher in the hope that they will give information about the children and be models for similar enquiries. They are also intended to generate conversation amongst the children so that throughout there is both a growing self-awareness and a sense of involvement.

The Workbooks are but starting points and the teacher may want to devise further material appropriate to his or her children. Time so spent will be well spent. It will pay richer dividends in the long term than formal and impersonal activities. Priority should always be given to the involvement of the child in language learning in concrete and active situations. Where the frustrations of failure have stunted or killed interest, then interest must be stimulated no matter for how brief a time. Many of these interests may stem from the impingement of mass-media and will flicker briefly in the window of the child's mind. If we are prepared to protect these flickering glows of apperception we shall succeed in helping the child to grow, to assert himself and 'to connect'.

[1] *See 'Teacher' by Sylvia Ashton Warner (Secker & Warburg), a fascinating account of teaching children to read, by finding their own particular words, in New Zealand.*

39

The interests of girls and boys

Throughout this book we have spoken of the child as 'he' for the sake of simplicity but all that has been said applies equally to girls. Boys are perhaps disadvantaged in our infant schools by the absence of men with whom they may identify and in whom they may see substitute 'father-figures'. Many boys who exhibit behaviour problems and, therefore, learning problems, come from families in which the father's rôle lacks adequate authority and they consequently find 'sex-typing' difficult. Girls similarly need to identify themselves as feminine but equally need paternal influence. Whilst both boys and girls can identify the quasi-maternal rôle of female teachers in infant and junior schools there is reason to suppose that they benefit from the presence of men on the staff and that boys, who are beginning to assert themselves by rejecting feminine characteristics and seek independence and a masculine rôle, benefit particularly by being able to recognise that the demands made upon them by school are not inimical to their masculinity.

There is little doubt that girls tend, in the main, to be more conforming and acquiescent to school than boys during the primary stage of education, although most classes exhibit some remarkable deviants from this stereotype. Perhaps this accounts for the fact that, usually, girls more readily adjust to school and settle down to learning to read. But, although at fifteen we usually find more retarded readers among the boys than the girls, it should be remembered that girls are then, in general, more mature than boys. If we allow for differences in maturational ages the differences between the sexes in reading ability are slight. The boys are often more noticeable for other reasons.

The language development of girls also usually advances more rapidly than boys' in infancy but again there is a considerable levelling out later. That the drives and rôles of girls and boys are different and that school requires different and greater accommodation from boys than from girls is perhaps the greatest single factor affecting adjustment by boys to the learning situation.

In determining the subjects to be used in the DATA scheme careful thought was given to the problem of producing books which would appeal to both boys and girls. Girls will read boys' books but the reverse is rarely true. Few men read in that remarkable genre, 'Romance', which lines the shelves of Public Libraries; few boys read the school, ballet and nurse stories specifically written for girls. In order to provide opportunities for girls to identify with characters in the stories, it was decided to place girls in central positions in all the stories. The titles of 'Zig and Zag from Planet ZV7', 'Zag the Great and Zig the Big' and 'Rik and Kara' make this explicit. It was not considered necessary to differentiate between the interests of girls and boys with 'Told by an Arrow' or 'The Data Book of "Joe Miller" Jokes'. The two 'Bruff' books, 'A Dog for Jerry' and 'Trouble with Bruff' have been found to be particularly appealing to girls because of their interest in dogs and puppies. In both books Jill, Rod's girl friend, provides an opportunity for the girls to identify with an adolescent girl.

At first sight 'Data on Cowboys' and 'Dead Man's Trail' appear to be essentially for boys but, in fact, the horses which play a strong part in the appeal of 'Westerns', are of such absorbing interest to girls that the books have been found to fascinate them. 'Dead Man's Trail' introduces romance, in the relationship between Jane and Ed Fox, in such a way that girls will detect more significance than will boys in the sub-plot. Young women are central characters in two of the three stories in 'Once Upon a Space' and the man-woman relationships are clearly established. 'Fly Away Paul' develops the theme of an adolescent boy-girl relationship and, although the story concerns itself largely with Paul's chase, this relationship was deliberately placed as the frame within which the action takes place; Alison, the other female character in the story, also provides opportunity for identification with a woman in a man's world, and Paul's attitude of respect for her is seen as a part of his growing maturity. 'In Fact' contains a number of sections specifically for girls interested in fashion, make-up, food, the 'facts of life', athletics, animals, etc.

However, whilst everything possible has been done to make the scheme attractive to girls it must not be forgotten that girls are interested in boys and the delineation of the characters of the boys and the illustrations have been made with this in mind.

41

5 *The Design of Data*

Within the context of the principles and considerations already described, the DATA scheme was conceived from the outset as a series of books which should have the maximum appeal to the children for whom it was being produced, should have built into it as many elements to maintain and develop their interest as possible and should have the highest standards of typography, design and illustration in order to contribute to the effectiveness of the books in helping children to develop both the basic and higher skills of reading. This resulted in a number of decisions which may not be at first apparent. For instance, the tastes and value-judgments of children are not necessarily those of adults, whether they be teachers or parents; and the tastes and values of children are not necessarily best met by subscribing fully to them. This is as true of books as it is of food. Arriving at the 'sense of the mean' is not always as simple as it appears.

Typography

Of the typography of children's books Sir Cyril Burt has written:

The most pressing need, therefore, is for all the various specialists to get together —teachers, psychologists, oculists and typographers—and endeavour to understand each other's point of view; it will then no doubt appear that there are a large number of urgent problems calling for experiment and co-operative research, in which each of the different experts will join and to which each of them will contribute from his own practical knowledge and experience.[1]

So far as it was appropriate and possible, this has been the approach used. Thus, in determining the typography of the books, we have been largely guided by the results of Sir Cyril Burt's own findings both as to typefaces and type sizes[2]. This is why sans serif typefaces have not been used except in the Workbooks. A number of teachers have commented on this with some surprise. But letters in sans serif faces, which lack the 'finishing touches' or scrifs of other typefaces, although they approximate the script or print used by infants, are the least easily recognised by children. This is not surprising as the word 'Ill 'in sans serif type becomes 'Ill'. However, it was thought desirable to use a sans serif type, Grotesque, in the Workbooks as a large point size could be used throughout the series, partly to allow adequate space for children's writing, and as, with a low density of print, it was appropriate to use a typeface which would help children with their writing.

The problem presented by the typography of the series was that of determining between the demands of legibility, i.e. readability, aesthetic considerations and children's reactions to typography. It is one thing to know that a certain typeface and size is easy to read and quite another to persuade children that they should read it. Children, like adults, have their pride, and it had to be recognised that children of 12 and 13 years of age would react against books set in jumbo-sized type no matter how easy it might be to read. They would rather be

---

[1] '*The Typography of Children's Books*', *Cyril Burt, in 'The Year Book of Education; 1960', Evans Bros. Ltd., London, 1960.*
[2] *Details of the typefaces and sizes used in each book in the Data Scheme are given in Appendix D.*

seen reading a comic or paperback set in 6 point! Throughout the series the typefaces have been varied and progressively reduced in size and, in order to avoid an impression of excessive juvenility, a compromise has been made between the maximum and minimum sizes of type considered desirable. Similar considerations have determined the lengths of lines and the spacing between them, but all the books have been given wide margins so that the appearance of each opening presents a relatively small 'reading load'.

Lines

It has become common for reading books for young children to be printed with lines which are not justified on the right-hand side and to vary the length of lines—ideally with the sense and cadence of the text. Because of the association this form of printing has for children with primers, however, it was felt advisable to limit it to the early books only. In DATA 5, 'Zag the Great and Zig the Big', free verse is used and variations in line length arise naturally, whilst in DATA 10, 'Data on Cowboys' the use of unjustified lines appears to result from the demands of the illustrations: in fact, the reverse is true as, in view of the bigger vocabulary load in this book, it was considered desirable to use unjustified lines to assist readability.

Maturity and variety of design

The 'Bruff' books, it will be noticed, are designed as typical books for older junior or lower secondary children. Coming as they do in the middle of the series and designed as they are primarily for top juniors and the younger secondary child, these books needed to have an appearance which would neither deter the immature eleven-year-old nor repel the thirteen-year-old. All the later books in the scheme have been designed to progressively approach nearer and nearer to the appearance of adult books.

It would have been far simpler to have produced an attractive uniform set of books and it is appreciated that teachers would have found this more convenient in use. The needs of the children, however, have been given paramount importance. If we are to stimulate children to read and avoid the impression that learning to read is nothing more than laboriously progressing through a set of uniform primers, then we must consider the growing maturity and changing interests of the children and provide with each book a new stimulus. The children for whom the books have been designed associate their failure with sets of primers; they certainly need continuous remotivation to tackle new and possibly harder books. For this reason each book has been individually designed and the covers, sizes, shape and thickness have been varied. The exceptions are, of course, those books which carry on and develop, quite deliberately, characters and subjects already established: the two 'Zig and Zag' books and the 'Bruff' books which are concessions to the desire to 'read another book like that other one I read'.

The illustrations for the books were commissioned on the understanding that realism, clarity and vividness were essential; that the art-work should aid understanding and increase the visualisation of what had been read; that it should stimulate the desire to read rather than remove the necessity for reading; that it should appear to have been executed for children older rather than younger than those for whom it is intended. The author is indebted to the artists for the considerable trouble they took to achieve these ends, particularly as in every case they had to subordinate their own natural desire to produce art-work which appealed to their own sensibilities to the need to find a style which would appeal to children.

The result, so far as the appearance of the books is concerned, is that they look much harder to read than they really are, and it is for this reason that we have given a brief outline of some of the factors involved. Experience in a large number of schools suggests that the initial reaction of teachers is that the books are 'too old' or 'too difficult', whereas the initial reaction of the children is to pick a book up, begin reading it because it appears attractive or interesting, and then to settle down and read it. This was precisely the intention.

The lay-out of each opening of the books, as has already been mentioned, has been designed to reduce the density of the print and, as the series progresses, this has gradually been varied. However, the first double-opening of solid print does not appear until Data 14, 'Once upon a Space', in which pp. 56 and 57 are the only unbroken pages of print. The last book in the series, 'Fly away Paul', is the only book to contain a few groups of consecutive pages unrelieved by illustration. By the time children have read the series, therefore, they should be able to read without the stimulus of illustration and be undeterred by grey pages. Reading should have become an autonomous, self-rewarding activity. This, too, is precisely the intention.

The cybernetic principles of design

The control of typography, including the omission of all ligatured letters (e.g. fl, fi, etc.) from the early stages of the scheme, the lay-out, line length and illustrations have been conceived not only as means of making reading easy but to arouse, maintain and develop interest both in the language and the content of the books. The illustrations in particular provide a context in which the children may read and visualise what they have read whilst extending the meaning and relevance of what has been expressed so that the child's participation in the book is increased. The principles underlying the approach used in the DATA scheme are explored by Karl U. Smith and Margaret Foltz Smith in 'Cybernetic Principles of Learning and Educational Design'. They point out that illustrations attract and hold attention and thus provide perceptual motivation:

> On the other hand, perceptually motivated behaviour is of little use in the learning situation unless it advances understanding of the subject matter. Thus visual material must be selected to direct and regulate the ongoing participation of the reader in such a way as to promote effective learning. Using illustrations in this way might be called *nonverbal prompting*, and it is especially valuable in difficult or complex material where pictorial displays keep the reader oriented toward the important points and help to structure his understanding of the subject matter. New concepts are better understood if they are defined by nonverbal as well as verbal patterns.[1]

For retarded and reluctant readers the 'nonverbal prompting' of the illustrations is as important as their ability to attract and hold attention. The illustrations expand and extend the significance of the text, promote the understanding and interiorisation of what has been read

[1] *'Cybernetic Principles of Learning and Educational Design' by Karl U. Smith & Margaret Foltz Smith, Holt, Rinehart and Winston, New York, 1966.*

and involve the reader in the subject matter; at the same time they help to maintain interest, aid visualisation and provide a visual check which the child can apply to his understanding of the text.

Seen in this way, the illustrations provide the teacher with a ready means of introducing children to the books for they may be talked about and discussed before the books are read without destroying the purpose and reward of reading. Similarly, when a book has been read, children may be asked to talk about the situations depicted in the illustrations and their understanding of the text assessed. As the series develops the art-work changes from the pictorially realistic to the more impressimistic style until in Data 17, 'In Fact', more sophisticated and abstract styles are used.

The comic strips beloved by children, and much-maligned by teachers, communicate by the vividness of the cartoons into which the dramatic action is compressed and use words only as *verbal* prompts ('Next day . . .') or as sound-track ('WHAM!' or 'Look out!'). If we reduce reading to this level we can certainly communicate both information and pleasure but we will not be increasing or improving literacy. Only by reversing the process and using language in print, into which the dramatic action or information is compressed, and by using illustrations as non-verbal prompts, can we aid children in their mastery of reading.

6 *Compounding Interest*

The interests of children, whether transitory or persistent, derive not from the objects of their interest but from their needs. In considering the interests of retarded and reluctant readers it was necessary to seek those most related to the basic needs of children of the ages with which we are concerned and, at the same time, to avoid creating in our minds a stereotype of a 'retarded reader'.

It also had to be recognised that even if it were possible to accurately delineate 'interest ages' this would seriously limit the use of the books in the early stages of the scheme with those older children who are more than two years retarded in their reading. In any case, one of the basic needs all children feel is the need to grow up. The high-grade mongol girl of seventeen wants to dress as a young woman, the thalidomide boy of seven plays at being a pilot. The retarded reader of 14 projects himself into the future, in his imagination, and dreams of the motorcycle he will buy with his wages. It seemed in every way desirable, therefore, to provide in each book as wide a spread of interests as possible so that the younger children's aspirations would coincide with the active interests of older children and to do so in such a way that, unlike the primers and school books to which they are accustomed, the books would appear to be for children older, rather than younger, than themselves.

Multi-dimensional interest

The principle of multi-dimensional interests to meet the needs of the various ages, both actual and developmental, of children is similar to that developed to accommodate the differing needs of girls and boys. Thus, the jokes in DATA 13 are for the most part well within the interest range of children aged 9 to 12 years, whereas the cartoons reproduced from 'Punch' give the book an appeal to older readers, including adults; the riddles and conundrums on each page are designed to attract and sustain the interest of the youngest readers in terms of maturity of interests, whilst the end-papers of Drury Lane and Joe Miller provide a context for the whole book in which it becomes acceptable for the more sophisticated and mature child to enjoy reading 'chestnuts'. Similarly, all children can be assumed to know something about Westerns but by no means all are interested in cowboys *per se*. 'Data on Cowboys', therefore, stimulates interest visually both by detailed, realistic pictures and by impressionistic illustrations; and provides for a wide range of interest by treating in some depth such subjects as horses, cattle, clothes, fires, blizzards, farming, history, windmills and the railroads. The orectic—emotional —development of children, their need to master fear, control emotions, adapt to and adopt value-judgements of society, their concern for loyalty, courage and self-reliance, is fostered by placing the cowboy, 'a man with guts and a horse', as the focus of interest. 'Data on Cowboys' is an exploration of the activities of man in the past and thus is rich in historical and human interest.

Multi-racial social influences

The changing nature of our own society is reflected in a number of the books in the scheme. We have already referred to the mediated experience children enjoy in our 'electronic global village' through TV which is used in the Odyssey of Zig and Zag. But today's children are also growing up in a society which is multi-racial and very different from that presented in the subtopias of the old primers. Moreover, in many of our schools, children who have learned English as a second language need books which will do more than simply provide them with opportunities to exercise the basic skills of reading. Their need is not for books which hypothesise a stereotype of an Indian, Pakistani or West Indian child written in a synthetic 'basic English' but for books which reflect the real world in which they live and which enrich their experience of our language. Indigenous children, too, need books in which children of other nationalities and races are presented as people. It is not so long ago that children's popular literature—and much adult literature—portrayed caricatures of bearded Russians as spies, Central Europeans as anarchists with bombs in their pockets, Africans as loyal bearers, Indians as loin-clothed assassins and American negroes as valets liable to break into a tap-dance. We have not come very far from those days in our popular culture.

The Data books attempt to reflect our multi-racial society: Rik and Kara certainly are not Western Anglo-Saxon Protestants; American Indians are portrayed in the two 'cowboy books', Data 10 and 11; 'Once Upon a Space' presents a wide variety of races and nationalities and the story, 'Day of the Doom', tells a simple allegory of a ghetto; a West Indian scientist is a central character in 'Fly Away Paul', whilst 'In Fact' deals with human problems in an international context.

Curiosity and the 'doctrine of interest'

The ground-plan of the Data scheme, so far as the interests of the children in the 9-15 age-range are concerned, is to provide a broad spectrum of interests and to reflect the world in which the child lives. Clearly, this is too generalised a view to have relevance to the individual child. Nor should we fail to recognise that the interests of young and immature older children are concrete and that, therefore, we cannot assume that the girl interested in her dolls or the boy with his model cars or trains is interested in reading about them. Similarly, the teacher who finds his fourteen-year-olds keep pigeons may well find that books about pigeons are no substitute for the real thing. The teacher of such a class found that the only way in which the interest in pigeons could be developed and used in the classroom was by helping the boys to write letters to arrange races and to assist in the recovery of lost pigeons. A visiting HMI was perturbed to find the blackboard filled with a model letter ending 'Yours in the fancy' but the boys were in no doubt that this was the register of language appropriate to the situation!

Despite the prevalence in our schools of 'the doctrine of interest' there has been remarkably little research which penetrates sufficiently deeply into the analysis of children's interests relevant to their needs in the reading situation as opposed to the concrete situation. What is clear is that children respond to living, moving and growing things, that novelty intensifies interest and that, as they develop, children begin to explore intra-personal relationships at first to discover their identity and later to discover their rôle in relation to others. Throughout, curiosity and exploration are the impulse. The need to classify and order, which is so dominant in children of junior school age, is reflected in their interest in collecting; the need of the adolescent to understand personal relationships and to identify with the peer group is manifest in the interest shown in 'Peg's Paper' type stories and the ubiquitous transistor permanently tuned-in to the same wavelength.

What we have attempted to do is to reflect basic and universal themes rather than specific interests which are more properly concrete and particular to the individual of a particular age, and to present them in ways which heighten and extend their significance either by means of novelty or by exploring detail. The need for detail is inadequately understood by many teachers both in their teaching and in their story-telling. Because children are preoccupied with the concrete rather than the abstract, only detail can provide a simulacrum of reality and satisfy them that the experience of the story, whether it be a fairy-tale, myth, legend or piece of 'derring-do', an event in the past or in a distant land, is significant, is 'real'.

One further point needs emphasis. The natural exploratory drives of children are best harnessed by being directed into their environment. Aborigine children, of course, do not need to go to school to do this. They can 'discover' all day long. Advocates of an 'environmetalist' approach to education, however, might ponder why it is, that despite such strong motivation, aborigines failed to discover the wheel or the artesian-well. A developmental approach uses the motivation of need and curiosity stimulated by a rich environment but directs experience into the richest seams and all the time stimulates language and intellectual interaction between the child and teacher. Unfortunately, many of our retarded and reluctant readers live in environments to which the only natural reaction is a desire to escape but to which they have become inured. They have adapted to it, like the aborigine, in order to survive and have learned to stay within its limitations. An American educationist Charles G. Spiegler writes:

> My major premise here is that culturally deprived youngsters limit their horizons to the four walls of the home, the four corners of the neighbourhood, and, as with many of my boys, the six pockets of the pool table. Television is their new window to the world. Through it they find the fullest, richest array of new interests man has ever known. . . .
>
> My minor premise is that interest is the key to reading. My conclusion follows naturally. Television, by creating interest, can become the road to wider reading.[1]

Using TV as the deprived child's new window

Children who see on television tigers 'burning bright' in the jungle, sharks roaming the depths of the sea or the birth of a baby may live in environments which are bleak and barren and but a testimony to man's degradation of his planet and of men. Let us at least recognise that the child can see through that 'new window' in his home to a richer and more significant world in which he wants to participate.

That many of the books in the series, and their presentation, reflect interests continually being stimulated by television is a result of our concern that they should be books that use as starting points the 'nowness' of the mediated experience the children have enjoyed. The books develop and enlarge, inform and give words to their experience of the world seen through the 'new window'. The relevance of the books to this experience is immediately apparent to the children in the 'Zig and Zag' and 'cowboy' books, 'Once Upon a Space', 'Fly Away Paul' and 'In Fact'.

[1] *'Give him a Book that Hits Him Where He Lives' by Charles G. Spiegler in 'Education of the Disadvantaged, a book of readings', Edited by Passow, Goldberg & Tannenbaum; Holt, Rinehart & Winston, New York, 1967.*

A book that hits him where he lives

Spiegler's own research into what culturally deprived children in Chicago demanded from books is as sure a guide as one could wish for. In summary, this is what he found his children wanted:

1. Books about animals, jobs, hobbies, sport, the sea, westerns; with adventure, excitement and facts.
2. Books that don't 'write down' to them just because they are poor readers; they've already 'had' the primers.
3. Good pictures, plenty of them, and big print.
4. Books written in a straight, direct, compelling style.

All the teacher has to do is to know the child and to seek and find the book which measures up to those criteria and which reflects the child's deepest preoccupations and, in Spiegler's words, 'hits him where he lives'. The Data books attempt to measure up to these demands but the wise teacher will know when and how to use them and to extend the child's reading beyond them. They are but aids and, like all aids, will best serve those who understand them.

One aspect of growing self-awareness in the developing child is that of his sense of belonging to a community. The child's name and address assume importance in that order. Throughout the Data scheme, both in the books themselves and in the Workbooks, we have referred to as large a number of places, villages, towns, cities, counties, regions and physical features as possible in order that as many children as possible will enjoy the surprise of meeting by chance a reference to places they know—something which we as adults also enjoy.

The Workbooks provide a variety of ways in which children's interests may be identified and in which interests may be developed. Teachers will be able to think of further applications and extensions of them. Above all, it is essential that we know the individual child's needs and inner drives and this we can only do if we are actively involved with the child in real situations. Schonell's recommendations, in 'Backwardness in Basic Subjects', [1] of nineteen activities involving oral expression preparatory to writing are relevant here.

[1] *'Backwardness in Basic Subjects' by F. J. Schonell; Oliver & Boyd, London, 1942.*

But there are other ways in which language, and through language our knowledge of the child and the child's ability to think and express himself, are best developed in our schools today. The less structured the situations in which children are involved, the richer they are in experience which penetrates all the senses. The more open-ended the paths we allow them to follow, and the more we are attentive to the child's questions than to our own, then the more able we will be to direct experience and to discover and satisfy the true needs of the children. Our classrooms need to be studios and workshops, resource areas and information stores, base-camps from which we set out to explore and to which we return to examine our samples, briefing and report rooms, conference and recital rooms, staging and observation platforms, and libraries which are talking shops. In such a situation there will be no need to resort to chronologically or developmentally arranged check-lists of interests: the children will be growing in thought and language, skill and confidence. Their interest will be compound interest.

7 Reading Language

One of the strangest phenomena in education is the language used in books especially written for children to learn to read. Whether it be 'The cat sat on the mat', 'Look, look, the ball' or the grotesque attempts to write in the language children are supposed to use, there is an artificiality about the language which immediately places the child in a strange situation. The reason is obvious enough. The moment we attempt to write according to a formula, whether it be based upon word-frequency counts or upon phonic structures, we are forced to write in a language which doesn't exist. It is equally difficult to write for children if we are dominated by the demand that each new word be repeated thirty times and it is far better to use children's rhymes and jingles, nursery rhymes and comic verse, which are known to the children and are essentially repetitious, than produce the monotony and unreality of 'primerese'. It is easy enough to smile at the results but young children eager to read suffer little harm providing they quickly master the decoding principles and can move on to more natural language, as the majority do. For the older retarded and reluctant reader the unreality of the language, once it has been re-trieved, is but an additional stumbling block. For this reason we have urged that for them and for all children the more natural and effective development of initial reading skills should proceed from spoken language to recording, from recording pictorially and symbolically to recording in print and that, thenceforward, writing and reading should develop simultaneously. Many successful infant teachers have done this for many years.

Reading as consolidation of skills

The problem still remains that, once children have mastered the initial skills, we wish them to read books which will not make them insecure but will gradually and successfully increase their mastery until they develop the higher skills of reading. Moreover, we want them to learn to read and to learn from reading. If retarded readers are deficient in language how important it is that they should increase their knowledge of language through reading. In his article 'Teaching the Mother Tongue to Backward and Subnormal Pupils', R. Gulliford rightly stresses the importance of learning by reading:

> The importance of language development for reading has often been stressed. The reverse effect of low reading attainment on language growth has equally to be considered since it cuts a child off from one of the main sources of general knowledge and vocabulary growth, as well as of the awareness of sentence patterns for the expression of ideas.[1]

If this is our concern, then we must be sure that what we give the children to read develops their awareness and familiarity with language as it really is and not in a synthetic form. Moreover, we require language and vocabulary which the children will understand, leading to language and vocabulary which will increase their understanding and experience of language.

The first function of reading for the child should be the exercise and consolidation of the basic skills of reading which the child has learned through his writing and the games he has played in associating patterns of phonemes with patterns of graphemes. G. R. Roberts and E. A. Lunzer conclude their study of 'Reading and Learning to Read' by observing:

---

[1] *In 'Educational Research' Vol. 2, No. 2, Feb. 1960, N.F.E.R., Newnes Educational Pub. Co., London.*

Indeed, it can be argued that most of the component skills involved in reading can be taught and should be taught independently of the reading of text. The latter serves the function of practice and consolidation as well as providing an end for activities of the former sort.[1]

Reading print must be seen as the end of the process of learning the skills of encoding and decoding language and as a consolidation and exercise of those skills. The purpose of books is not, then, to teach children to read but to exercise, develop and extend the skills of reading as a self-rewarding experience.

It is for this reason that we have assumed an initial 'reading age' of about 7·5 years for retarded readers although, in fact, the first two Stages of the scheme were successfully tested in typescript with infants aged approximately 6·5 years. The progression of difficulty in most reading schemes is too steep for children whose language or skill is deficient and it is a common experience of teachers to find that half-way through many schemes of primers supplementary materials from other schemes have to be used to help the children. This gives rise to 'platform' reading, a system used in some schools whereby the children are required to read books from two or three different schemes at approximately the same level of difficulty. In one well-known and otherwise excellent series at the very point at which children are meeting for the first time long and short vowel digraphs ('each' and 'head') they are also expected to cope with expressions such as 'overwhelming urge', 'responded to the demands', and 'rejoiced at his success after such an unpromising start'. For many children this may present little difficulty but for many it will be but obfuscation. The problem we have endeavoured to solve is that of providing a long and gentle gradient of difficulty with a high level of interest. To do this it is essential to use real, easily understood, direct language and to use the non-verbal prompting of illustrations to support it and to extend its significance, to help reduce uncertainty and increase comprehension. It was also considered vital to encourage over-learning of phonic and structural patterns and to use a style and

[1] 'Development in Human Learning', edited by E. A. Lunzer & J. F. Morris, Staples Press, London, 1968.

subject matter which encouraged identification, involvement and impulsion to read on. In reading, the motivation must be provided by the message.

The register of printed language

One factor which is insufficiently recognised and which presents difficulty to retarded and reluctant readers is that there is a difference between spoken and written language. When we speak we are behaving in a situation common to our listener and ourselves and can rely upon the fact that situation and gesture, intonation and emphasis, all contribute to our behaviour being understood. When we write we must make a conscious effort to create a situation and rely solely on the words we use, and the ways in which we arrange them, to communicate. When we read we must make an adjustment to the situation implied in the text, whether it be a novel, a letter or a newspaper report, and we rely upon the cold print to trap our thoughts and carry them along. Listening to speech our attention is held physically and meaning is conveyed by tone and emphasis. Possibly the words are entirely superfluous as we receive the message from the person's expression which may be merely facial but may be with the whole body. Or 'I hope to see him there' may signal '*I* hope to see him there '*I hope* to see him there', 'I hope to *see* him there', etc., and express a whole range of feeling from complete indifference to intense anticipation. Retarded children may well react correctly to the situation without the words registering. With only the printed words to inform them they may be completely at sea or accept them at their literal meaning. Again, whilst the language of the middle-class child may approximate the elaborated code of written language it is, nonetheless only an approximation. No one speaks as he writes and we write as we would read. For children whose language environment is poor the difference between the spoken and written forms of language is so great as to represent a real barrier between them and understanding. Only frequent opportunity to listen to adults read will help them to become familiar with the written registers of language. But this problem does place upon writers the responsibility to write as directly and explicitly as possible and in a style which is close to spoken language.

Writing for reading

Writing for retarded and reluctant readers is not a restriction upon the skill of writing: it is an incentive to write well. Sir Herbert Read, after quoting Piaget's dictum that 'The line of development of language, as of perception, is from the whole to the part, from syncretism to analysis, and not vice versa', said of the sentence:

> The sentence is a single cry. It is a unit of expression, and its various qualities—length, rhythm and structure—are determined by a right sense of this unity.
>
> Sentences in their variety run from simplicity to complexity, a progress not necessarily reflected in length: a long sentence may be extremely simple in construction—indeed, *must be* simple if it is to convey its sense easily.
>
> Other things being equal, a series of short sentences will convey an impression of speed, and are therefore suited to the narration of action or historical events; whilst longer sentences give an air of solemnity and deliberation to writing.[1]

True children's writing, which results from deeply felt experience and heightened perception, has this 'right sense' of unity and a directness and pace which immediately rings true. It is only when we encourage children to clutter their writing with adjectives and adverbs that they lose the speed of events and the clarity of reality. The writer for children, particularly the writer for retarded and reluctant readers, will find his models in the writing of children and in all good writing which cares for the right word and economy of expression, which avoids elaboration and decoration and which concentrates upon the concrete. Those are the qualities we should look for when seeking books[2] for children. We will find it in Conrad's 'The Secret Agent' but not in his 'The Nigger of the "Narcissus" ', in Defoe, Swift, Fielding, Charlotte Brontë, Dickens when he isn't filling out to the next instalment, Mark Twain, Hemingway when he remembered Gertrude Stein's advice that 'remarks are not literature' and in George Orwell, if we need touch-stones. We will find it in C. Day Lewis' 'The Otterbury Incident'. We are not likely to find directness and vividness in 'award-winning books, written by aunties for aunties.

Throughout the Data scheme we have aimed at directness and

[1] *'English Prose Style' by H. Read, G. Bell & Sons Ltd., London, 1963.*

[2] *See 'The Ordinary & The Fabulous' by Elizabeth Cook (Cambridge University Press, 1969) which examines versions of myths, legends and fairy tales suitable for children.*

simplicity but have developed the length and the depth of the structures and language used as the scheme progresses. At the same time the style attempts to reflect the content. Thus, in 'Data on Cowboys', the repetitive nature of the style is used to convey a sense of the rolling sea of the plains; in the allegorical 'The Day of the Doom', in 'Once upon a Space', the style is clearly different from that of the previous story; 'Fly Away Paul' is told in the first person and this allows a more colloquial style than would otherwise have been possible. The use of 'free verse' in 'Zag The Great and Zig The Big' permits the use of repetition, rhyme, alliteration, assonance, variations of rhythm and typogrammes, and thus provides a vehicle for the reinforcement of clusters, letter patterns and the sight-sound relationships which are so vital at this stage in reading. It is also hoped that the various devices used will encourage children to write rhymes and jingles and to play the 'language game' with wit and skill as well as to explore the emotional use of language, rather than its scientific use, in Coleridge's sense, and discover and express something of themselves beneath the thin carapace of intellect.

But if we have been concerned with a 'unity of sense' and a unity of form and content in our writing, we have also been concerned with the control of vocabulary and with providing a sound linguistic base upon which the children may develop from the basic to the higher skills of reading.

Graphemes, phonemes and morphemes

Children who have learned the basic encoding-decoding of language into and out of print, whether by learning to write and to read what they have written or by prodding through primers or using reading apparatus of one form or another, are still insecure in the skills. They should know that print is encoded language, understand directionality and the sound-word-meaning relationship. But they will still need help and practice in developing the automatic skill of recognising graphemes (*kn/ee*) as phonemes (*n/ē*) and synthesising these into a morpheme (*knee*). No matter by which method children are taught to read, alphabetic, phonic, linguistic, i.t.a., whole-word, colour-coded, Gestalt 'look-and-say' or 'mixed method', it is usually at this

60

stage that they need the most help. They may recognise '*elephant*' but confuse it with '*telephone*', fail to differentiate between '*pat*' and '*bat*' or '*bone*' and '*done*', still be unsure of blends such as '*st*' and '*str*' or diagraphs such as 'f*ur*' and f*ir*', and need help with 'ambiguous' letters in words such as '*s*ugar'. They may recognise the morpheme '*live*' but have difficulty with the allomorphs '*lived*' and '*living*'. One problem, basic to all of these difficulties, will be that of scanning the word to determine the correct combination of letter strings and the syllabification of the word. If we imagine a child attempting to 'build' the word '*pigeon*' ('*pig*'-*e*-*on*', '*pige*-*on*', '*pi*-*ge*-*on*' etc.) we appreciate how much uncertainty he must eliminate before he arrives at '*pij-in*'—unless, of course, he has been prompted to anticipate the word by teacher or picture.

Clearly, we need to provide frequent exercise of the most common clusters of letters and this we have done. But the poor linguistic endowment of many retarded readers gives rise to other problems. Not only is their speech poorly articulated, often it is incorrectly articulated. Not only is their language structurally restricted, often it is incorrectly structured. No matter how liberal our views may be about 'correctness' of articulation or appropriateness of language, many retarded readers are inefficient communicators by any standards. There are a variety of ways, of course, in which these children are helped in school but it appeared to be in every way desirable that they should be helped in the process of learning to read. Failure to do so results in their failure to learn to read.

Function words

If we listen to the speech of many children we notice that not only is the language limited and often inaccurate but that words are run together so that it is difficult to distinguish between, say, the article or possessive pronoun and the noun. 'Upt'road' and ''znoone's in 't'ome' are common. If we look at a typical account written by a child we notice the large number of small words that are used:

There was this man and he pulls up in his car and puts his head out of the window and he calls me over to him and says, 'Can you tell me the way to the station?' So I points down the street and tells him to keep straight on until he gets to the cross-roads and then to turn to the left and he'll see the station straight in front of him.

Most of these small words, often elided in normal speech, are particles which are used to relate one thing or event to another. Particles or function words constitute about 30% of written English and often account for over 50% of spoken English. They are variously named, 'grammatical words' being another term used for them, and variously defined. If we remove all the nouns, pronouns, verbs, adverbs and adjectives then we are left with 'function words': the articles, conjunctions, prepositions, exclamations, the WH-words we use in questions, response words such as '*yes*' and negators such as '*no*' and '*neither*', modifiers which extend the significance of verbs as in 'sit *up*', and qualifiers such as '*very*'. These 'little words' are nearly all morphemes which are unchanging in form but have a wide variety of functions, e.g. *up the hill, rode up, Road Up, catch up, speed up, pull up*. Because of their importance in English and their frequency it is essential that children know them and see them in all their 'nudity' detached from the words to which they play a subservient but vital rôle. In speech many function words are unstressed and elided, as we have seen, but in reading print our recognition of them must be automatic. Detached as they are in print they *reveal* the nouns, verbs adverbs and adjectives, which are more commonly stressed in speech and which carry the information. As soon as we generate sentences beyond the simplest kernel form (*Boys run*) function words are necessary (*Some of the boys run to the river and then look back.*).

The function words are uniquely suited to establishing the links both between sound and sense—because they are simple morphemes, and between graphemes and phonemes—because they introduce them in frequent and simple words (*the, this; a, an, and, etc.*), and also because they provide opportunity for the retarded reader to progress from the recognition of frequently recurring letter 'strings' to frequently recurring word 'strings' (*over and over again*).

If we now add to the function words the pronouns (*e.g. she, her, hers, her own, herself, whose, which etc.*) and the various forms of the auxiliary verbs (*Have, Do, Be*) we have a large number of frequently recurring morphemes which introduce a large number of phonemes (*th, sh, ch, etc.*) and a very large number of frequently recurring word 'strings', (*e.g. he did not have, she may have it, they will be there, it would have been very . . . etc.*). All these words, once known, assist children to recognise both sound-sense units combined in other words ('*thing*' *and* '*some*' *in* '*something*') and syllabification (*an, other another, mother, brother*).

Many of these words (*e.g. the*) are not phonetically consistent or vary in pronounciation according to the stress placed upon them (*e.g It's and It is*!). But this is by no means a disadvantage: print is but an approximation to the sound and the sooner children begin to adjust sound to meaning the sooner they will be able to tackle more difficult words. Throughout, our emphasis with retarded readers should be upon print and 'sound-sense' rather than just upon print and sound.

The first pages of 'Told by an Arrow' use these 'little words' almost exclusively and throughout this book they are continuously exercised. With the illustrations as non-verbal prompts to assist in the decoding of the noun and predicate phrases, the children are able to concentrate on scanning for sense at a low level of reading difficulty. The identification of 'sense units' and syllabification is also encouraged by using the phonemes of a word in other words. The word '*arrow*', for example, is not only repeated but its sounds are echoed, in whole or in part, in the following words: *arrows, narrow, narrows, shallow, bow, show, low, blows, blowing, follow, sparrow, crow, know, slow, slowly, Harold, etc.* In this way we are not merely reinforcing the word itself but, much more importantly, imprinting the habit of recognising the significant components of words and of making adjustments to those components, where necessary, to arrive at the certainty of sense. Reinforcement by extension and transfer is both more efficient and meaningful than meaningless repetition.

In all of this, it will have been noted, we have endeavoured to proceed from the pattern of language, to the pattern of words, to the pattern of sounds and of letters. Our concern for pattern arises both from the nature of language and the nature of learning. The retarded reader will be helped if he is encouraged to consciously look for pattern. The able reader sees ISLANDAHEAD and immediately sees the pattern of letters which make the words. He can distinguish between ISLANDAHEAD! and ISLANDAHEAD? He is unlikely to read it as 'Is L and A head?' The retarded reader needs to play at changing the patterns by changing the initial letters, the vowels and the ends of words (*band, land—bend, lend—bark, lark*) and encouragement to distinguish between the common phonemes in both reading and writing. This we have provided in the Workbooks and this phonic aspect of the scheme is set out in Appendix B. But the books and Workbooks, it is again emphasised, are but aids. Some children will not need to read all the books, nor will they need to work through all the Workbooks. Others will need help before they tackle the books or supplementary exercises to develop the necessary and appropriate skills presented in the Workbooks. The more the teacher can make a game of these exercises or relate them to some other purposeful activity, the more successful he will be in helping the child. As reading is concerned with meaning, everything the child does should be both successful and meaningful.

Because the function words are so frequent and so significant and because they introduce the syllabification principle (e.g. *into*), they foster the recognition of the graphemes as phonemes which make morphemes and allomorphs (*in, into, indeed, index, indoors, infant, inform, ink, instead, instruct, intend, interest; to, today, tomorrow, tonight*). Children who have mastered them are well on the way to reading. If they are helped by the non-verbal prompts of illustrations and given the additional vocabulary they will need by their teachers they will learn to read by reading.

High-survival-value words

Besides providing a matrix of meaningful sense-sound units we have introduced, at the beginning of the scheme, a number of words which we need to recognise in order to survive. Words such as 'Danger', 'Poison', 'Stop' and 'Warning' need to be recognised by the illiterate if he is to survive today and if we can only teach him to write his own name and address and recognise HSV-words our time will have been better employed than had we succeeded in getting him to learn a primer by heart.

With illiterates learning to pass their driving tests by recognising road signs only by their shape and colour, we all have a vested interest in ensuring that all children recognise HSV-words and understand their significance. These words are among the first that retarded readers should know—not only in the interests of their own safety and of those they may put at risk, but also because they are continuously being reinforced by the signs they see in town and country. Reading is a self-rewarding *social* activity, we have said, and we need no stronger evidence than the HSV-words to convince retarded and reluctant readers of this fact. HSV-words place print firmly in a social context and they, too, 'hit the child where he lives'.

Particular words

Whatever subject we write about we must use words particular to that subject. Whatever limitations we impose upon our vocabulary, whether of phonetic simplicity or of high-rating in word-frequency counts, these must be subordinated to the demands of our subject. We cannot, for example, write about football without using words such as 'match', 'referee', 'goal', 'centre-forward' and 'off-side'.

Throughout the Data scheme, therefore, we have used the words appropriate to the subject matter wherever they were necessary. 'Told by an Arrow' and 'Data on Cowboys' are obvious examples of this. It was also considered desirable to avoid reducing language to vague generality in the interest of simplicity: to do so makes reading for older children a boring and unrewarding activity. Instead we have endeavoured to particularise and provide sufficient detail to arouse and maintain interest and to relate to subjects and interests with which, it was reasonable to expect, children might be familiar. It would have been adequate, for instance, to have written, in 'Told by an Arrow', '*Arrows from the English long-bows beat the French*' and to have left it at that. But, by adding, '*at Crecy and at Agincourt*', although we increase the difficulty of reading by the use of the two 'particular words', we are communicating information which directly relates both to the subject and to what children will know about, no matter how vaguely.

If the words prompt the children to ask for help with them the teacher has the opportunity not merely to tell them what the words are but to talk to them and to interest them in books and pictures which will tell them something more about 'Crecy' and 'Agincourt'. Our purpose in helping children to read is not that they should plough through 'reading books' but use books as tools. This aspect of reading is further extended in the Workbooks. As teachers we should not underestimate the value of these activities nor the ability of children to engage in them. We may not be zoologists but, if the need arises, we will readily turn to an encyclopedia to find out about the glyptodon. Having done so we will still not be zoologists but we will have gained whatever information was appropriate to our level of understanding. Children are perfectly capable of doing that and, just as we do, of gaining other information in the process—for example, that 'glyptos' is the Greek for 'carved', hence 'glyptics' for gem-carving, hence the fluted teeth, etc. As language is the tool which changes us as we use it, so using books as tools changes us.

Particular words are also introduced early in the series to provide children with a familiarity with the names in print of the countries, continents, oceans and planets of their universe. Whether they are familiar with them or not as a result of their schooling is immaterial: they are bombarded by them by the mass-media. This latent knowledge needs to be conscious knowledge and to be organised. The Workbooks contribute to the beginnings of this process and help to advance retarded readers towards the goal of involving them in the mainstream of education.

The importance of mathematics for retarded readers

The language of mathematics is the language by which man describes and defines the spatial and quantitative aspects of his universe and establishes relationships between them. Today we are recognising that children are born into a three-dimensional world and that it is not merely the quantitative and computative aspects of mathematics which are important to them. Infants now explore cylinders, prisms, spheres and pyramids and, in many schools, will

66

talk competently about rhomboids and parallelepipeds, symmetry and rotation. Directed experience will have familiarised them in Junior schools with the associative, commutative, conservative, distributative and reversible properties of number. They will have mapped, used Venn diagrams and set theory to classify and establish relationships; they will have recorded in block charts, pictograms, pie charts, graphs and histograms. In real situations they will have developed an understanding of mathematical concepts and acquired the language and the beginnings of the logic of mathematics.

Both mathematics and science today provide the open-ended situations in schools in which children can explore and grow in experience and in language. Retarded readers whose language is poor and who have perceptual and conceptual difficulties, who find classification and the discernment of relationships and of patterns difficult, will benefit more from rich experience in science and mathematics than from being prodded through lateral print. In the activities of exploring their environment through mathematics and science there will be abundant opportunities for them to grow in language and understanding, to record in signs and symbols and to learn the encoding-decoding skills.

Within the confines of the Workbooks it has only been possible to provide limited experience in these activities. It is impractical to prompt children from a Workbook to engage in open-ended activities. Such activities are the proper province of the teacher and arise from his or her relationships with the children in the context of the learning situation he or she devises. Books which list 'Things to do' or 'Now try this' and assume that the children are surrounded by microscopes, balances, compasses and thermometers at the moment they happen to be reading, or urge them to get up and do some pond-dipping, are remote from reality, to say the least. We have limited our prompting to those which may reasonably be followed up by children in a normal classroom provided with a modest 'library' of reference books. An atlas, encyclopedia such as 'Pears' and an AA book is about as basic as could be imagined!

But the teacher is not as limited as the writer of Workbooks in the activities he or she may devise and, whilst it is hoped that teachers will experience no difficulty in making the few provisions for the children to follow up those which have been included, there is no doubt whatsoever that the children will benefit most from open-ended directed activities in mathematics and science in which their language and thinking, their experience and understanding, will be developed. Through them they will learn how to learn and to find for themselves a feasible world and their identity in it. It is this experience and understanding which will inform their reading; for reading is not the passive absorption of coded information but the interaction of thought encoded in print with the thoughts and feelings of the reader. This is made explicit in the 'In Fact' book which explores a wide range of subjects in such a way as to involve the reader'sthoughts,imagination and critical faculties, no matter where he may begin reading, about himself, his species, his past, present and future in the 'nowness' of his real universe.

Skill drill or PAOCK

Because reading is an internalised activity, it must be automatised. We have already indicated the attempt we have made to introduce phonemes as morphemes in the function words and to draw attention to significant letter strings or clusters (*str*, *-dge*, *-ea*, *-ei*, *etc.*) and common word strings. Each stage in the series stresses particular graphemes which are exercised both in the texts and the Workbooks and are set out in Appendix B. Teachers will note how word-attack skills are developed in the 'Car Number Games' and in 'The Sound's the Same'. However, no attempt has been made to teach spelling by rules as these are often so complex and riddled with exceptions as to cause confusion. The simpler rules of spelling are well within the competence of any literate adult (doubling of final consonants, 'i before e except after c', etc.) and teachers will know when and how to teach them. The rules which govern, for example, the spelling of -R- and -RR- words such as 'preferred' and 'referable' or -ABLE and -IBLE words such as 'collapsable'/'collapsible' are beyond the needs of retarded and reluctant readers and are, at best, not rules but the codification of convention.

A further difficulty about the phonic aspect of language is that not only are there considerable local variations but we are rarely conscious of the subtle distinctions which do exist when we say, for instance, '*th*' in '*thin*' and '*those*' or the '*o*' in '*mode*' and '*mote*' and in '*theory*' and '*violets*'. We accommodate these variations within the sound and graphic patterns with which we are familiar. It is usage which produces variations, not the alphabetic code. When we read, the graphemes prompt sound responses which we synthesise into words which have contextual meaning. Roberts and Lunzer (*op. cit.*) described reading as a 'hierarchical process of uncertainty reduction in which the key level was the identification of words'. It appears appropriate, therefore, to concentrate the attention of the retarded reader on common consonantal and vowel graphemes he meets in words rather than to confuse him with spelling rules which are both abstract and complex. In this way we can encourage the automatic recognition of and response to them in a meaningful way.

The children will be helped in this considerably if they are given some drill in writing the common words in which the clusters or strings occur. Today drill is unpopular although pianists, violinists, singers, typists, footballers and golfers persist in it. Perhaps if we resort to some such euphemistic euphuism as 'a programme for automatising orthographic conventions kinaesthetically' (PAOCK) it will prove more palatable!

Handwriting is a skill which has to be automatised and by the use of writing patterns, such as those of Marion Richardson, children acquire both the neural circuitry and physical dexterity necessary. Consequently, when the skill is used they find it easier to write 'qu' and 'se' than to write 'qb' and 'kp' which are impossible in English. If children are encouraged to write words containing the common graphemes and letter patterns they are developing the skill of handwriting and imprinting the sequence of letters kinaesthetically. If, at the same time, they subvocalise, so much the better: it is doubtful if it is physically possible to stop them doing it subconsciously and, therefore, better if they do it consciously. In this way the skill of handwriting and the skill of spelling progress in harmony. The handwriting should be clear and flowing and progress to elegant fluency so

69

that it really is an efficient automatic skill. For this to be the case the child needs the same progression as the typist learning to 'touch type'. The child who starts writing with, say, Marion Richardson patterns learns the directionality of print from the outset; he learns, too, the basic shapes and the ligatures that join the common clusters. And these simple tasks require and improve concentration. Like the typist's, the progression should be from those common clusters, such as 'oo', 'ee', 'co', 'ea', 'th' and 'fr', to common words which contain them. Note that the typist does not practise typing 'qw' or 'zx', although the keys are next door to one another, but concentrates upon clusters she will meet in language, such as 'qu' or 'zo'.

The various lists of words in Appendix B provide ample opportunity for this type of drill and it is suggested that retarded readers will benefit from regular but brief five-minute spells of writing a line each of four or five words containing the same graphemes and then writing two or three times a sentence containing them. Clearly this should be a pleasant and purposeful activity and not a superfluous mechanical one. The words chosen may well be those with which the child is not fully familiar but which we wish to make familiar. It is important too that, if he needs it, he should be given models in his exercise book, rather than on the blackboard, to copy, and that the teacher should be sure that he is writing the letters from the right starting points and executing them correctly: if this is not done he will be reinforcing error. Left-handed children will need help because without it they will cover up what they have written. If their paper is tipped down to the right and they use a higher hold on their pencil than is normal this problem will be overcome. Ambidextrous children will be encouraged to use their right hands and clumsy children to relax their grip and to use a larger, bolder hand. For all children posture and the distance between paper and eye is important.

A child experiencing difficulty in decoding words containing *'age'* and, who perhaps spells them 'phonetically' as *'idj'*, for instance, may be helped by writing a line each of the words *village, message, voyage, bandage*, followed by a sentence in which the words are used—*'On the voyage they received a message asking them to take bandages to the village'*. In this way the pattern of letters is experienced kinaesthetically in a meaningful context and will be more readily recognised in print and remembered in writing. Whether we call such experience 'drill' or 'PAOCK' is immaterial, the benefit to the child will be that of familiarity with the patterns of letters and the progressive reduction of uncertainty. As adults, when we are not sure how to spell a word we try writing it. We must train in this facility so that the children we teach will have automatised the skills they need.

8 *Retardation and Reading*

Retardation in reading is a relative and imprecise term. Sometimes retardation is used in the context of a description of a disability as when, for instance, we speak of a deaf child whose language development is retarded; here it is clear that the child's language development has been held back below the level of children of the same age. When we speak of retardation in reading it is generally assumed that we refer to a level of reading ability below the child's potential which is assumed to be average or above average for his developmental age. To be more specific we often hear retardation expressed as a difference of levels of attainment: John is said to be 1 year retarded in reading if his Reading Age is 12 years and his Chronological Age is 13 years, although we would make some allowance if he were considered to be 'young for his years'. We are unlikely to know a child's Developmental Age, as this involves measuring the maturity of his skeleton, but we may well know his Intelligence Quotient or Verbal Reasoning Quotient. If we do, then we may give an impression of scientific precision to our statement by saying that John has a Mental Age of 12·5 and a Reading Age of 10 and is 2 years 6 months retarded in reading. Which would not appear very surprising but could be very misleading. Let us look at the true story of Celia.

Celia was six, had an assessed I.Q. 50 and could not walk, crawl, talk or feed herself. She was diagnosed as suffering from cerebral palsy and her condition was described as spastic quadriplegia. Every movement she attempted caused spasms which sent her arms, legs and head jerking violently. Her days were spent strapped in a high chair. As she was considered ineducable she could not be admitted to a residential school for cerebral palsied children. A home-tuition teacher was asked to try to teach her and ascertained that Celia responded by grimaces to what was said to her and laughed when her teacher grimaced back. From this simple communication system the teacher developed a code of responses and a range of sounds which approximated speech. In six months Celia attained a 'primer age' equal to her actual age and a Word Recognition Age of 6·9 years. Her I.Q. could still only be assessed but Celia could read, was deemed educable and admitted to a residential school there to achieve her one ambition—to walk.

Locked in the mocking cage of her body, Celia had had no ascertainable potential. The teacher established interaction between them and turned an illiterate, ineducable, physically handicapped child suffering from brain damage into a literate and educable child. Clearly, we need a better definition of retardation, a better understanding of potential, 'intelligence' and 'reading age'.

Retardation defined

In this book the term retardation has been used to describe reading disability which results from a failure in the interaction between the child and his environment. It is used to distinguish retardation from 'backwardness' which may be more properly described as reading disability which results from deficiencies or dysfunction within the child and beyond our intercession. The distinction is important. Educationally Subnormal children, for example, may be described as 'Backward in reading' rather than retarded when everything humanly possible has been done to educate them. Our intercession may give specialised teaching and hearing aids to the partially hearing, glasses to the partially sighted and Braille to the blind; if, when all that we

73

can do has been done, their disabilities do not allow them to read as well as they might otherwise do, then we may describe them as backward in the skill.

The reasons for defining retardation, which is also a matter of degree, as reading disability resulting from a failure in the interaction between the child and his environment, may still not be clear. The first reason is that we cannot assess or predict with any degree of certainty or accuracy what a child's potential is because children do not develop intellectually at a constant rate nor is their intellectual development solely the result of innate abilities.

A child's development is the result of the interaction between the child and his total environment; physical, intellectual, emotional, cultural and social influences interact with one another within the child. Intelligence is a capacity which has to be developed like strength, which develops in spurts of rapid change and periods of slow growth like height, and which, like weight, is not constant. Intelligence, like the state of our health, is variable and our health, general well-being and emotional state affect our intelligence. In the words of the Plowden Report: 'Thus the notion of the constancy of the I.Q. is biologically self-exploding—as well as educationally explosive.'

Language and intellect

As the language development of children is inextricably a part of their intellectual development, measures of their intelligence reflect their language development. We know that non-readers are non-scorers on group verbal reasoning tests; that the measured intelligence of identical twins brought up in disparate cultural environments, say one with Kalahari bushmen and one in Shepherds Bush, reflect the effects of their different circumstances; that the average I.Q. of children of professional parents is over 20 points higher than the average I.Q. of children of unskilled workers, and that this difference is usually attributed to the differences of language used in their homes.

The definition of retardation in reading which we have given is applicable to socially and culturally deprived children. Their disabilities in reading, if they exist—and they may not, of course—are the result of deficiencies in their environment which have failed to provide the stimuli and the language necessary for their development. Throughout, whilst not ignoring the primary needs of children for love, food, warmth and protection, we have placed language central to the needs of the child for his intellectual, emotional, social and cultural development and central to the educational process. Culturally deprived children who are failing in reading are not backward readers: they are retarded readers.

'*Reading Age*'

The second reason for this definition of retardation is that we should also regard with equal caution the concept of 'Reading Age'. Reading is an acquired skill and is in no way related to age. You have either learned to read or you haven't. The highly intelligent girl of five who has learned to read may not be reading Wittgenstein but may well be reading 'Winnie the Pooh', whilst her friend who cannot read may well be reading tomorrow, next week or next term. All that matters is that a child should be able to read and want to go on, and have the encouragement and opportunity to go on, reading. Measures of 'reading age' are merely measures of language development *and* reading experience in our schools. We cannot tell whether the child who fails to recognise 'colonel' or 'scintillate' lacks the words in his vocabulary or the ability to decode them. He might do better with 'lieutenant' or 'scincoid' if he is in the school orchestra and has played 'Lieutenant Kije' or keeps lizards.

Nor can we accept that reading skill is better assessed by reading comprehension tests: again we are unable to test reading without testing vocabulary and language structures. None of this is to suggest that such tests may not have their purpose as coarse classificatory or screening devices in schools but they are inadequate for and irrelevant to an accurate definition of reading retardation. Moreover, they are suspect on other scores. Tests which were standardised thirty or more years ago should, in all conscience, underestimate the abilities of children today who are developing more rapidly and under more favourable social and educational conditions. Certainly, they often encourage an atmosphere of complacency, as evidenced by the D.E.S. report 'Progress in Reading, 1948-1964' which, when all was said and done, merely assured us that we were up to pre-war levels of literacy, more or less. The danger implicit in this situation is that we may well be underestimating the abilities of the generality of children and failing to recognise the true extent of retardation present in the child population.

We only recognise human potential when that potential is realised and it is in the nature of man to be immediately challenged to strive to go beyond it. Whether the ultimate limit be the four-minute-mile or getting to the other side of the moon, we are never satisfied or complacent. Reliance on 'Reading Age' may reinforce complacency and be about as useful and scientific as weighing children with little green apples and using them year after year.

Ages in cages

All the shibboleths and the measures we customarily apply and use in education are now the subject of the most rigorous examination, often by the very people who first elaborated them.[1] Invariably, the results of their original research were never fully understood nor applied within the context of the qualifications they delineated. Too often over-simplification and generalisation has been the order of the day. We have been to some lengths to explore the problem of the inter-relation of intelligence, language development and reading ability and to highlight some of the reservations it is necessary to make about an over-simplified and glib definition of reading retardation which reduces it to an equation. But let us remember that it is only in recent years that we have begun to look more closely at Chronological Age and have recognised the simple fact that 'summer-born' children are both younger and have a shorter time in their infant school, that they often found themselves in the lower streams of junior schools or all lumped together in 'unstreamed' classes. Groucho Marx once described American education as 'ages in cages'. We still find it convenient to think and to organise in ages, ability groups, streams, sets, subjects, and to apply labels when we should be observing the child and studying and responding to his needs.

[1] *See, for example, 'Intelligence and Cultural Environment', Prof. P. E. Vernon, Methuen, 1969.*

The importance of high expectation

To return to Celia. It would have been understandable, if unforgiveable, if her local education authority and the home-tuition teacher had deemed her ineducable and lacking in potential. She was enabled to get the physical education she needed by learning to read. Today there are in our schools hundreds of thousands of children who, because they are not thought to have the potential, are denied the opportunity of enjoying the cultural and intellectual education they need. They may not have to win their right to learn to walk by learning to read but they have yet to be helped to learn to learn. Frequently they are underachieving because they are not expected to achieve. They have been weighed in the balance and found wanting and only now are we realising that perhaps the balance was wrong. If we will assume that the potential is there and recognise that it is the function of education to develop it by finding the appropriate interaction then we may well overcome the handicaps of both nature and nurture.

Invariably in dealing with retardation we fail to go sufficiently far back to the stage in the development of language or of the skills of writing and reading at which the child is competent and completely secure. Invariably we do not continue aid and support until the child has developed those skills sufficiently. To go forward it is often necessary to go back and, having gone back, we may still need help and encouragement to follow the path through the jungle. Interaction between ourselves as teachers and the child and between the child and his total environment, his peer group, his family and all the influences operating upon him, all need to be in harmony if the child is to achieve maximum 'operational efficiency'. They rarely are, but the school is the one conditioned environment within the control of the teacher.

Interaction between child, parents and school

It is increasingly recognised that the attitude of parents can be the most potent single factor influencing the development and attainments of children. It would be strange if it were otherwise. The mother conceived the child, expected it to be born, expected it to be weaned and to cut its teeth, expected it to talk and to walk and expected it to go to school. And there, in many cases, expectancy ended. In the past

77

some schools encouraged the belief that interaction between parent and child might be positively deleterious! 'Don't interfere—leave her to us and all will be well,' was a common reply to parents with the temerity to enquire about methods of teaching reading. Often the same schools believed in 'reading readiness' and the 'wallpaper approach to reading' which assumed that if the children were surrounded with books they would one day discover they could read them.

For a long time good schools, recognising the natural and vital rôle of parents, have involved the active interest and informed support of parents in the development of their children in adapting to school and in learning to learn. This again is only as it should be. But the best schools have always had a more positive rôle than this. They have seen themselves as catalysts in their communities. They have not been content to accept the attitudes of parents but have set out to change the attitudes, where necessary, for the good of the children. Such schools give the disinterested parents a new respect for their child and, often, a new interest in and respect for themselves. These schools see not only the influence of the parents on the child but the influence of the child upon the parents. In these schools the children are fulfilled and have a place and a purpose; the children find their identity, self-respect and a sense of achievement which enhances them and, through them, their parents. Such schools do not accept the negative influences of the environment and of the parents but mediate between the child and his environment and moderate the attitudes, standards and values of the parents.

Successful schools are concerned for two things: for the needs of the children and for excellence. They are effective in involving the children in what they are good at and in excelling in what they do. From the strategy of success they strive to attain excellence by the tactic of short-term realisable goals. These schools are not the microcosm of the macrocosm of society, reflecting society's sub-standard standards, but catalytic agents interacting with society. In practical terms: if there are no books in the homes then the children will be taking them there. If the language of the home is poor, then the children and the school will enrich it. This is what education has always been about. The school is not a repository for the children of problem families but the environment which creates the parents of tomorrow. It leaves little time for testing and demands a testing time for interacting. Interacting in a successful school will not be achieved if the retarded readers are isolated to receive remedial education as this will only produce restricted education, restricted experience and a restricted code of language. The failures will find heroes in the drop-outs and their rôles will be supplied by the rejected.

If we have always accepted as teachers the importance of the interaction between ourselves and the child, and are now re-learning the importance of interaction between parent and child, we have still to explore the interaction of child with child. The Opies[1] have explored this interface in the secret language of children and successful schools have begun to explore the ways in which child may educate child. As in ethology we have recognised that we cannot study animals in zoos but must observe them in their natural habitats, so we must recognise that we cannot study 'ages in cages'. If schooling is not to be an interruption to children's education then the school must be an environment which provides successful interaction between children and children, children and their parents, children and their teachers, children and culture. Again we are only applying in a social context the cybernetic concept of interaction through feedback.

---

[1] 'The Lore and Language of Schoolchildren' (1959) and 'Children's Games in Street and Playground' (1969) by I. and P. Opie, Oxford University Press.

9 *Reluctant to Read*

It is understandable that retarded readers are often reluctant to read. The true reluctant reader has the ability to read but no inclination to do so. Many children who are reluctant to read, if not detected, may become retarded readers. In the early stages of acquiring the skill anything which creates an antipathy to reading, whether it is the difficulties encountered in reading or teacher and parent attitudes to the child or to reading, may generate reluctance.

The reluctant reader has received inadequate attention and reluctance to reading is often too glibly dismissed with the blanket advice to parents and teachers that all one has to do is to find what the children are interested in and give them a suitable book which, it is blandly assumed, they will read. This advice assumes that reluctance is overcome by interest and that the best way of pursuing interest is by reading. Apply the advice to reluctance to eating cabbage or to a skill like swimming and we realise that the advice is not only an over-simplification of the situation but begs the question. Reluctance is the symptom and not the disease.

Degrees of reluctance

Reluctance, like retardation, is a matter of degree. There are degrees of reluctance which extend from revulsion to simple indifference. There is a world of difference between the boy who regards books as 'a load of rubbish' and the work of 'egg-heads', on the one hand, and the boy who is so keen on sport and all the activities in which it involves his waking and dreaming life that he never opens a book.

The degrees of reluctance may be defined as: revulsion, repulsion, resistance, reluctance, disinterest, and indifference. The measures we adopt to overcome reluctance will clearly be different according to the degree of reluctance. The reluctant reader has to be brought to the position of being susceptible to influence, re-orientated to reading and remotivated. It follows, therefore, that the teacher must not merely determine the degree of reluctance but can only proceed from a knowledge of the child and his circumstances in depth, must be *en rapport* with the child, and that his concern must be for the child and not for the peripheral skill of reading.

The child who finds reading repugnant is not going to read a book simply because parent or teacher suggests it is interesting. If the child is interested in animals he may well resent books simply because they come between him and the physical contact he needs with animals. It is perfectly reasonable to love listening to music but to have no wish to read about it. And how often do we read the books we are recommended to read by people for whom we have no regard? It may well be that encouragement to read an interesting and suitable book is but 'negative reinforcement'. The approach to some reluctant readers might well be more successful if they were told 'I'd rather you didn't read this'. Some would be sure to read a book they had been told not to open on pain of death. Forbidden fruits are used to sell a wide range of commodities from cars, through holidays abroad to turkish delight but, too often, persuasion in the classroom is as subtle as a sledge-hammer. We will apply Occam's razor before this line of arguments involves us in the dangers or advantages of censorship!

Arthur was a boy who could read but never read. He was not just a reluctant reader who found books repugnant: life was repugnant. At the age of eleven he had already lost his father, and had mourned him for a year, and he knew his mother was slowly and painfully dying. He lived face to face with tragedy, suffering and in poverty. School was irrelevant to his predicament; his teacher's sympathy was rejected with contempt because it was powerless to give him back his father or to save his mother. He sat silent and scornful or flared into anger and violence. His teacher, a wise and compassionate man, recognised with humility that all he could do was accept him as he was. From time to time each day, Arthur buried his head over his exercise book which was never handed in. With one arm round the book, his head down, Arthur slowly wrote. His teacher made no comment. He wished Arthur could lose himself in a book and find some escape or comfort. But Arthur never read. Then one day he handed in his exercise book with the rest of the class. Spring had come, Easter was near and the children had written about them. When the class had gone home the teacher turned to Arthur's exercise book. Carefully written in Arthur's still unformed hand was a poem headed 'Easter'. It was the most corruscatingly corrosive plaint of hate and despair the teacher had ever read, a poem as incisive in its imagery as a poem by Baudelaire or Rimbaud. It was Arthur's 'black manifesto', a statement of rejection of all that his teacher represented. The exercise book was filled with poetry, uneven in quality but consistent in its intensity. The teacher did not write on the book. He slipped a copy of Wilfred Owen's poems into Arthur's desk. They never spoke about them. 'The poetry is in the pity.'

Reluctance as 'work paralysis'

There are many children whose emotional and social predicament, whilst not so tragic as Arthur's, is nevertheless such that school is irrelevant or antipathetic. This is not the fault of the school but of circumstances outside it. Moreover, the children may not posses Arthur's gift of refining feelings into highly articulate expression. Their rejection of life or of school and their teachers is expressed in resistance, rebellion or indifference. Their inarticulateness results in their showing their feelings by their attitudes and their behaviour.

82

We cannot hope to reach them by arranging book displays, talks about interesting books and sets of glossy 'work cards'. Certainly they will be no more susceptible to exhortation than to programmed learning.

The older reluctant readers in our comprehensive and secondary schools are often in a state of what Erik Erikson[1] has called 'work paralysis' when we would have them in a condition of active 'apprenticeship'. Some will have prematurely fixed upon inappropriate rôles or be confused about their sexuality, others will be in rebellion against authority or seeking leadership, or confused about social and personal values. Few will have found a true identity. Today the pressures of the peer group are heightened by commercial exploitation of teenage 'pop culture' which presents a mirage of fulfilment in a real world which is here and now. Certainly it is real enough but its effect is to foreshorten the adolescents' concept of his future and to encourage the belief that he has arrived as an adult whereas, in fact, his childhood is being protracted. The subterranean language and mores of this society is as remote from the adult as the secret 'lore and language of school-children', but it is a human society, surprisingly rich in its diversity and its questioning, often more honest and direct than the world inhabited by parents, politicians and preachers. It is presumptious to imagine that an interesting book is all that is needed to turn 'work paralysis' into 'apprenticeship', to turn reluctance into eagerness.

Group interaction in attitude changing

Changing the reluctant reader and re-motivating him entails changing his attitudes to himself and to his world. We may do this only from understanding and only in conditions in which the child himself may re-orientate *himself*. Relaxed and informal discussion in which hearts and souls may be freely bared, and opinions and attitudes, standards and values, fears and hopes, formulated and examined, are more likely to succeed than anything else. In discussion the individual is not driven into an attitude of opposition and self-defence but has

[1] *Erik H. Erikson: 'Identity, Youth and Crisis', Faber & Faber, London, 1968, and 'Childhood and Society', Penguin Books, 1965.*

room to manoeuvre, to shift ground, to retract and regroup, to re-
formulate and to change. Here thought is not overwhelmed by the
wisdom and weight of years borne by the teacher but provoked by
the ideas and opinions of others in the same or similar predicament.
Once formulated, ideas are externalised and lose something of the
impulsion of emotion and subjective animus. The very act of seeing
what we think by hearing what we say may expose prejudice we did
not know we had and our confused contribution to discussion may
produce clarity in our thinking. The rôle of the perceptive and skilled
teacher who knows the virtue of his own silence is that of the sympathetic listener not of the questioner who, like Bacon's Pontius
Pilate, 'would not stay for an answer'. And it is the sympathetic
listener to whom we turn for understanding, confirmation and
approval. In this way the teacher does not change opinions and
attitudes but creates the conditions in which opinions and attitudes
change themselves.

Curiosity and the exploratory drive

The Head of a comprehensive school once told a new member of his
English staff, 'I'm giving you a form that has only a term to go before
they leave. I don't mind what you do—they've no interest in school
and only come because they haven't the wit to stay away. There must
be *something* in English that you can do with them!' The teacher
spent the first session getting to know them and the second listening
to them talk about what they intended to do when they left school. He
asked the Head if he had really meant what he had said and, receiving
reassurance, told him that for the rest of the term he wanted to send
the form out of school to work in the Reference Department of the
Public Library. The Head wished he hadn't opened his mouth but
acquiesced. The Chief Librarian was doubtful but couldn't refuse.
The boys were told that each would be given a notebook in the front
of which were some of the questions each had raised during the
previous discussion. They would spend the rest of the term finding
answers to these, and any other questions they were interested in, at
the Reference Library. There was just one condition: the teacher was
very busy and wouldn't be able to come with them so did they mind

looking after themselves—he would see them in the form-room before they left and when they came back.

Everything went well until a fortnight before the end of term when the Head sent for the nearly new member of staff. The Chief Librarian had rung to say his staff were very disturbed. The boys had told them they were leaving and no arrangements had been made for another class to come down. 'Said his staff were quite upset—it's the first time the Reference Librarians have felt they were doing the job they were trained for. You should think of these things and plan ahead.'

The boys had filled their notebooks. They had found some quite remarkable questions to answer and some remarkably interesting answers. They had been reading widely and really using books under expert and often most attractive guidance. The experiment had worked because the teacher saw that what these boys needed was trust and confidence, respect and self-respect. He had found their needs in the discussion and a way of finding answers to those needs. From that point on they were on their own in an adult world. And *that* was what they wanted.

Between the extremes of Arthur's tragic isolation and the reluctant class in a comprehensive school, teachers and parents will recognise many variants of degree and of causation. We must look closely at the emotional, physical, cultural and social needs and circumstances of each child and provide the conditions for change. We must recognise, too, the conforming children who religiously perform their work adequately in a state of uncomplaining boredom and futility and will leave the education system with certificates, O and A levels and degrees like stigmata to remind them of their boredom, and poisoned against everything our culture represents save worldly success. They, too, have failed to realise their potential and have worked in conditions of partial 'work paralysis'. Often they have overcome their repugnance at the expense of a paralysis of the spirit.

If we can determine the degree and cause of reluctance in our children then we are in a position to re-motivate them. Often, if reluctance has not been early detected, we would be well advised, as with retarded readers, to ensure that at first we encourage them to read material which makes little demands upon them. Often we are not

Mell, New York Herald-Tribune Syndicate. (Re

prepared to go far enough back in order of difficulty or far enough down in order of quality. Applied to adult books, it is often as if we expected the entire literate population to read only Shakespeare or James Joyce. If we want reluctant readers to start reading we must often be prepared to swallow our prejudices and find the simple book that 'hits the child where he lives'. We shall find this easier if we are continuously and incidentally introducing a diversity of books—and reading from them—in as many unexpected contexts as possible. Science teachers who take time out to read from a scientist's notebook or from 'Nature' or 'The Scientific American', and geography, history and mathematics specialists who will move from the safety of their notes and out-of-date textbooks to turn to original sources and contemporary accounts of significant past and present events and who, above all, have a sense of humour and of the surreal lurking beneath the real, will create the opportunities for the reluctant reader to see books in new lights. Perhaps one of these lights will provide the spark.

Humour, jokes, comic verse are more than release mechanisms. The child or class who can still laugh with the teacher, rather than at him, will accept suggestion and advice from him too. The reluctant reader who returns to reading to find that it makes him laugh may well find a new identity and learn to laugh at himself.

But there are some reluctant readers who, once their inner needs have been identified, will resent anything which smacks of the immature or trivial. During their abstention from reading their maturity may have grown and they would now prefer to respond to a challenge. If we have found what interests them we must have at our disposal a deep knowledge of the resources of literature which are available to us. The art master who left a recording of 'Death of a Salesman' on his desk was pestered by a class to let them hear it. Reluctantly he agreed to satisfy their curiosity. The class listened as it worked. At the end of the session some of the children wanted copies of Arthur Miller's play, others asked if they could hear some more 'plays like that'. As teachers we need a wide familiarity with books which enables us to

87

respond to opportunities such as this—and ingenuity to create them if they do not exist. We can only equip ourselves for this by reading with a catholicity of taste born of our own insatiable curiosity. If we are curious about the ways of man and our universe we shall be most fitted to stimulate curiosity in children and to direct their reading into suitable channels when their curiosity has been aroused. Reluctance, in all its modalities from revulsion to indifference, cannot withstand the itch of curiosity. And it is curiosity we must use, rather than transient interest, to remotivate the reluctant reader.

The conditions we create in our schools and classrooms will militate against reluctance if vitality and pace are our style, conversation and discussion our means of communication, interaction our way of life and the real world our oyster. In these conditions we will be involved with our pupils and a part of, rather than apart from, the real world. In real situations uncertainty, novelty, surprise and tensions arise and curiosity is provoked which triggers off exploratory activities and provides the drive to learn to learn. Curiosity is the grain of sand which, occasionally, makes pearls. The moments of significance and the reawakening from 'work paralysis', the arousal of curiosity and predisposition to change are the conditions we should continuously seek so that interaction between ourselves and our pupils may be effective in meeting their needs to grow and develop.

Once we have established these pre-conditions we should be able to give the child a book appropriate to his needs and within the competence of his skill which he will read with pleasure and reward. The variety of books in the Data scheme and the range of interests they cover, together with opportunities to identify with real people in real situations or to engage in fantasy, have been designed to assist teachers in meeting some of the requirements of reluctant readers. The Workbooks encourage the reluctant reader to seek other books and to use them in a variety of ways. For once reluctance has been overcome we want reading to become an accepted and habitual activity, an established pattern of behaviour. For this to happen, our pupils must be made familiar with the diversity and richness of the resources of books. This entails that our initial success must be quickly and effectively followed up.

It is only when we have learned by personal experience of them that books can amuse us, can give us information, vicarious experience or penetrating insights into our own minds and the minds of others, can enlarge our consciousness, explore the development of character and the unfolding of events, confirm or deny our certainties or prejudices and make us feel, imagine and think, that we begin to appreciate their richness and diversity. Only by reading books do we develop the ability to read with discrimination, to appraise what we have read and, gradually, to acquire taste and judgement. The development of the higher skills of reading is the development of the ability to contribute to a dialogue with the mind of the writer. As teachers we must help our retarded and reluctant readers to develop these higher skills so that this interaction of minds may take place.

From the beginning the children's experience of reading should engage and involve them. The Data scheme, it is hoped, will enable children to sample some of the varied pleasures and purposes of reading with success and confidence. As teachers we should continue to guide and encourage wide and wise reading until we can say to our pupils, in the words of Zarathustra: 'Now do without me!'

10 *Using the DATA scheme*

Although the Data scheme is designed to be used sequentially and, for this reason, progresses both in order of reading difficulty and in the maturity of interests upon which it draws, it is not intended that all retarded readers should start at the first book and work their way through the series. Both pupil and teacher have a part to play in determining where and how to start and how to continue.

The teacher who knows the child and his abilities may well be able to select the appropriate book and provide the incentive and support necessary for the child to read it. He will be better able to do this successfully if he is thoroughly familiar with the books and the levels of reading and comprehension difficulty to be met in each of them. To assist teachers to become familiar with the books, and with the ways in which the principles and considerations we have already described are applied, we set out in this chapter a brief synopsis of each book and its main characteristics. We also indicate the approximate level of reading difficulty of each Stage in the series by giving its 'Reading Age' but we would reiterate that this term has little to do with the sequential mastery of the decoding skills.

The pupil's part in the process of determining where to start in the scheme is of particular importance in the situation in which teachers sometimes find themselves when confronted by a new class or form of children, of an age-range with which they are unfamiliar, and in a school in an area which they saw but briefly when they 'went for interview'. In a situation such as this and when previous records of the pupils' abilities are unfortunately not available, the teacher may initially have to allow children to exercise unguided choice in the selection of a book. It is unlikely, if they are severely retarded, that they will select a book in the scheme such as 'Fly Away Paul' or 'Dead Man's Trail' which are full-length stories, although they may be attracted by the covers and subjects to look at the illustrations. It is more likely that they will select a book which interests them, some of which at least is within their competence to read and which is not a continuous story. Certain books in the scheme have been specifically designed to be read by a wide age-range of pupils having a wide range of reading ability. The books are: 'Told by an Arrow', 'Zag The Great & Zig The Big', 'Data on Cowboys', 'The Data Book of "Joe Miller" Jokes' and 'In Fact'. Each of these books contains sufficient simple material of interest and/or amusement to sustain the efforts of retarded readers to persevere with print. Trials in schools indicate that retarded readers who have failed to read simple primers will persist in their efforts to read one of these books although it may present them with a considerable challenge. By their own efforts, often prompted by pictures, sometimes seeking the help of friends or teacher, they succeed in reading much more than they have previously achieved.

If teachers allow children to choose their own books they may well be in a position to identify both the interests and reading abilities of a child and, armed with this information, be able to guide the child to a book which will prove less difficult but equally interesting. They may also be helped to identify a child's strengths and weaknesses in the decoding of print and use appropriate sections from the Workbooks to train out deficiencies. For this reason the graphemes exercised in each of the Workbooks are listed in Appendix C. Children who are given help in this way will appreciate its value and are usually ready to co-operate fully in a short, intensive attack upon a specific difficulty. They will also be disposed to accept the teacher's guidance in the selection of the next book they should read. If in this way they find success in reading they will need little encouragement to work their way through the rest of the series.

The diversity of interests which have been embodied in the scheme allow it to be used flexibly and in a variety of ways appropriate to the needs of the children. This is the essence of the developmental approach we have described and why the books and Workbooks should be seen as aids which teacher and child may adapt to their needs.

In schools with Remedial Departments or which 'set' for reading, DATA is often used as a 'core' reading scheme. In these schools the emphasis has often been on developing topics or 'centres of interest' around the subjects of the books so that language skills, the vocabulary and encoding-decoding skills, as well as the characters and situations, are established before the books are read. Similarly, before children move on to the next Stage in the scheme, they are encouraged to develop topics far beyond the limitations of the Workbooks, with the result that their language and intellectual development is accelerated. Children have pursued studies of the planets, space and London after reading the Zig and Zag books, have turned from 'Data on Cowboys' to write their own histories of the overlanders of Australia, and have found a new interest in handwriting and art after attempting the calligrammes in The Second Workbook. One school has developed its own 'About You' questionnaires so that the relevant information obtained from them can be fed to all departments after these sections of the Workbooks revealed that, amongst its retarded readers, were talents unknown to both the P.E. and Music Departments. A large comprehensive school discovered that 'Data on Cowboys' had aroused so much interest in American history that the book is now used in its History Department. In one form of another school the codes introduced in the Workbooks stimulated so much research into codes and ciphers that the pupils were surprised and delighted to find that they could decode the message in 'Fly Away Paul' long before Helen described to Paul the intricacies of the Playfair cipher.

But perhaps the saddest story we have heard, however, is that of the class of severely retarded children who were all drearily working away at the same page of the same Workbook. When a visitor asked if all the children were so carefully graded that they had read all the previous books in the series, she received the reply: 'I didn't know there *were* any other books'! Perhaps this incident underlines the need to know an aid before we use it as much as it stresses the need to know our children and to be sensitive to their needs. Here we, like the children, are in the hands of the teacher.

Stage One   *'Reading Age' 7-8 years*

> Data 1   'Told by an Arrow'
> Data 2   'Zig & Zag from Planet ZV7'
> Data 3   'The First Workbook'

Data 1—'Told by an Arrow'

The vital but largely neglected stage in learning to read, reading signs and symbols, is the starting point which gives retarded readers confidence and immediate success. Teachers may wish to extend this activity by drawing upon the environment of school or locality. The book aims to increase perception of signs and symbols seen at home and in the street and to establish that understanding and using them is 'reading': in terms of survival in urban society the signs and symbols cannot be over-estimated. Older children will be familiar with positive and negative and other electrical symbols; can they read a wiring diagram and do they know the colour-coding of electric cable?

The arrow is used to emphasise the importance of directionality and increase awareness of orientation. It is the most potent and universal of all symbols and its use with children who have hand-eye co-ordination difficulties is recommended. Teachers will find that these children are helped in their attack upon print if an arrow is used at the beginning of a line of print; in handwriting arrows will help to indicate the direction of strokes. Experience suggests that an arrow communicates more information than a cross (x) in this situation, the cross being static and merely capable of indicating a starting or finishing point whereas the arrow shows direction. Again, in using an arrow to help these children, it will be found that the fletching is best omitted and that only the shaft and point need to be used as this increases emphasis and reduces confusion.

'Told by an Arrow' exercises the function words (*on, over, in front of, behind, etc.*) and establishes their importance linguistically and phonetically as sound-sense units. If full benefit is to be derived from this book children should be introduced to it by being encouraged to discuss the illustrations: retarded readers should not be assumed to possess either the understanding or the vocabulary and structures necessary to interpret the situations depicted. Talking about the pictures will also provide opportunity for the introduction of the 'particular' words such as 'legend', 'Robin Hood', etc.

The later sections of this book, 'Arrows from the Past', 'Bows and Arrows from Afar' and 'The Bow and Arrow Today', are not merely to exercise reading skill: they show how a theme may be developed to relate to the total learning situation in schools and establish reading as a significant experience both in the everyday life of society and in school. Thus, these sections serve as a model of the type of extension which should be encouraged at all Stages of the Data series. This will ensure that throughout their development the children do not regard reading as an isolated and irrelevant activity which only takes place in 'reading lessons'; it will also ensure that reading is reinforced both in the street and in the school.

For slow-learning children the emphasis on road safety is quite deliberate: it is more important that they should know 'STOP', 'GO', and 'CROSS NOW', for example, than 'Look, look, the ball'. All children will be helped if they are encouraged to collect examples of the signs, symbols and words they see in their neighbourhood. Benchmarks, fire hydrants, warnings of hazards, street names, notices and advertisements abound which, once the children are made aware of them, will increase their understanding of their world, their ability to read and survive in it and, ultimately, *to contribute to it.*

Data 2—'Zig & Zag from Planet ZV7'

The problem was that of writing about the everyday world, which children may be safely assumed to know, in an interesting way. By the device of introducing Zig and Zag as visitors from another planet we have put the reader in the position of knowing more about the world than the visitors. Had we written about sea and water, grass and trees, the elements, seagulls and blackbirds, buses and roads, the seaside and funfairs, without this device we might have been reduced to the empty insignificance of a dead language. Again the aim is to heighten perception of the real world, to give success by placing the reader in the position of sharing a secret and to create the feeling of 'nowness'.

Descriptive writing has been reduced to a minimum and the illustrations, acting as visual prompts, assist internalisation and the automatisation of the reading process. Zig and Zag and their space-ship are not described and the artist has taken care to encourage identification by boys and girls with Zig and Zag by portraying them as 'other wordly' without making them grotesque. It should also be noted that the ages of Zig and Zag, as portrayed, does not inhibit identification by 'teenagers'.

The vocabulary, which includes very few 'particular' words such as 'radio', 'controls', because of the situation, is particularly rich in function words.

Teachers may wish in some instances to introduce this book by reading aloud the first few pages to the children in order to establish the situation. This may well take the place of 'talking about the illustrations' and leave the delight of discovery—that Zig and Zag are, in fact, very small—to be revealed in reading. Because the illustrations do not *tell* the story it is a simple matter to check that children have understood what they have read. Slower children will be helped by 'response reading' and the style of the book lends itself to this activity.

This book introduces simple conversation and 'called', 'asked' 'told' and 'said' are introduced on the first page. Some children may need help in the conventions of punctuation which signal direct speech. Special attention has been given to this in The First Workbook, in the section headed 'I said to him, I said . . .'; it will be noted that in Data 2, direct speech is also inset to assist children to recognise those occasions on which speech is carried over to the next line.

The typographical lay-out of the book, the use of typograms on p. 13 in preparation for their more intensive use in Data 5 and the

Workbooks, the colour and impact of the art-work all contribute to prompt the understanding and enhance the significance of the simple text. The aim of the book is to imprint upon the retarded and reluctant readers that reading is a self-rewarding activity.

When the book has been read teachers may quickly assess how much the children have understood by asking two questions: first, 'Tell me about Zig and Zag?' and, secondly, 'What were the giants making at the Fun Fair?' The first question is open-ended, the latter is 'closed' and permits of only one answer! 'Fun' is the impression the book should make upon the children.

Data 3—The First Workbook

The Workbook begins by requiring the children to record symbolically by using the arrow and gradually develops the ability to write sentences using the vocabulary and structures they have met in the first two books. Directionality is fostered but, it should be noted, from the beginning the emphasis is upon *reading* instructions and responding to them. Some children will need help in reading the instructions but, throughout the series, instructions have been used as an integral part of reading activity. Thus, in what appear to be simple 'sentence completion exercises', for example, we are primarily concerned with exercising reading and understanding: this is exemplified in 'Another Way' and in 'I said to him, I said . . .', where the appropriate response can only be made if the sentences have been understood. It is in this way that we have exercised the vocabulary and phonographs introduced by the books. Exercises such as 'All Set', in which children have to make up sentences from the 'prompt' of a group of three or four words, similarly require that the words can be read without a context and can be given an appropriate context by the children; this, of course, also involves the use of function words. All these activities, therefore, provide diagnostic indications upon which the teacher may build additional reinforcement activities.

'The Car Number Game' is used to develop word-attack skills and in this Workbook exercises the consonants and short vowels in particular; it will be noted, however, that modified vowels are involved in the '.or' and '.ow' examples, having been introduced in 'for' and 'North' and in 'bow and arrow', etc. This game is developed throughout the series and is used in a variety of ways. It is hoped teachers will encourage children to play it amongst themselves.

The phonetic and linguistic structures used in each of the Workbooks are set out in Appendix C, and we need not treat them in detail here. However, the stress in this First Workbook on 'Because', 'Right and Wrong' and high-survival-value words is not because of the importance of spelling them correctly: it is because of their importance in the cognitive development of children, in establishing relationships and causality, that they have been introduced right at the beginning of the scheme.

The two 'About You' sections have proved extremely popular with children. They encourage in children a sense of their own identity and increase their consciousness of themselves and their characteristics and abilities. It may be far more important to a child to be able to stand on his head or to learn to roller-skate or swim than to learn to read. The teacher who is prepared to help him acquire these skills— not necessarily by actually teaching them herself, although this is perhaps the ideal solution—will establish a relationship in which all things are possible.

The value of maps, diagrams, signs and symbols, has been stressed elsewhere in this book. The teacher who can use the Workbooks as starting points for further activities will reap the highest dividends.

Some of the questions in this Workbook appear at first sight to be best answered with 'Told by an Arrow', opened at the appropriate page, in front of the child. Pp. 30 and 31, for example, may be answered in this way. However, this is not the intention, and it is hoped that children will be encouraged to attempt these and similar exercises in the other Workbooks by trying to remember the answers. As teachers we frequently underestimate the retentive powers of children's memories and fail to develop them: the memory of many retarded readers, both visually and aurally, is best developed by being exercised. However, when children have attempted to answer these and similar questions from memory, they should be given opportunity to seek the answers in the book. This, in turn, will help to develop the ability to read for information, a facility initiated in the 'Facts to Find Out' section.

97

Data 4   'Rik & Kara'
Data 5   'Zag The Great & Zig The Big'
Data 6   'The Second Workbook'

Data 4—'Rik & Kara'

Although this book builds upon the vocabulary established in Stage One and develops the 'arrows' theme, its appeal to children is founded in the family situation and Rik and Kara's hunt for food. The 'low key' illustrations contribute to the atmosphere of the story and to an understanding of the text; this is particularly important in helping children to visualise the stages by which Rik invents his bow. The 'contemporary' appearance of New Stone Age Rik and Kara is by no means accidental and encourages girls and boys to identify with them; their ages are also deliberately set as 15 and 16, respectively, whilst their brother Lef is aged six and sister Tam is five, so that older retarded readers feel that they are reading about people with whom they can identify in a familiar family situation in which age carries responsibility.

The bow was man's first way of storing energy and teachers may wish to develop this theme and encourage pupils to find out about other ways of storing power, from clocks to batteries. Pupils will have little difficulty here but may well be seeing, for the first time, a new dimension of their world in a new light.

The direct, sequential narrative style is one with which children are thoroughly familiar: it is the way in which they relate events. However, as the story develops the narrative includes descriptions of events, such as lighting the fire and the search for game in the forest, which demand that the reader follows, with closer attention to detail, the relationship between cause and effect. At the same time, however, the vocabulary is extremely simple and the sentences are, for the most part, short.

The book may well be introduced by the teacher asking children to try to imagine situations in the New Stone Age when there were no shops, no roads and few people and by asking pupils to describe some of the differences in everyday life. This will assist pupils to project themselves, in their imaginations, back into the past. Alternatively, teachers may wish to read aloud to their pupils the first Chapter, which establishes the characters and the situation; in this way they may satisfy themselves that the readers are prepared to tackle the book, have had their curiosity whetted and are familiar with such terms as 'flint' and 'spear'.

The opportunities for follow-up, once children have read 'Rik & Kara', are considerable: some teachers may wish children to make their own historical enquiries, others may consider their pupils better equipped to use the story as a starting point for improvised drama. Both these approaches are to be preferred to 'comprehension' exercises. Certainly, the more conversation to which the book gives rise, the better.

Data 5—'Zag The Great & Zig The Big'

This book is self-contained and there is no need for children to have first read 'Zig & Zag from Planet ZV7'. The scene set in the earlier book is established in the first few pages of this book. Free verse is used so that alliteration, assonance, rhyme, lines of varying length, repetition, lists, and typograms may be introduced naturally and without betraying that they are but devices for increasing children's perception of print. The 'nowness' of television is also presented in a way with which pupils, accustomed to our 'space age', are thoroughly familiar—although this aspect of their world is sadly lacking from the vast majority of school books. Similarly, the book involves children in the global world with which television has familiarised them by switching rapidly from pole to Equator, from Mount Everest to the Nile, and from Planet Earth to Planet ZV7. Wherever it has been used, the response of children to this book has been one of immediate acceptance. Considering the diversity of subject matter and the use of free-verse, songs and jingles, this is perhaps surprising: certainly, it is a far cry from the books with which retarded readers are familiar and this suggests that we have been correct in our assertion that children do need books which reflect the influence of television upon their perception and understanding of their world. The illustrations play a large part in involving pupils in the adventures of Zig and Zag.

The use of rhyme has made it possible to establish a much larger vocabulary than is normally used in books for retarded readers which are dominated by 'reinforcement by repetition'. *'Scared—prepared'*, *'sky-scrapers—newspapers'*, *'in the Nile—crocodile'*, *'were soon—typhoon—afternoon'* are examples. But rhymes have also been employed in which the spelling is not consistent—*'head—wed'*, *'knew—clue'*, *'bore—floor'*, *'sure—shore'*, *'target—Margate'*, *'Jeff—deaf'* so that pupils are familiarised with the vagaries of our orthography and are also helped to recognise the variety of print-sound correspondence.

Follow-up activities from this book arise naturally as, having read it, pupils have a greatly increased awareness of their universe and of language. Some pupils have been encouraged to write their own rhymes, jingles and songs; others have investigated sounds because they had been surprised to realise that dogs can hear sounds unheard by humans; some have begun plotting news items on an outline map of the world, others to find out why a ring of light does appear in their TV screens' top right-hand corner—they hadn't noticed it before. All that need be said is that the opportunities for follow-up activities abound and do not need to be forced upon the children.

Data 6—The Second Workbook

A more rigorous approach to word-attack skills is developed in this book in both 'Printers' Errors' and 'The Sound's The Same'. Also, there is both a heavier reading load and more activities, such as 'Who was First?', which involve the use of information books and atlases. And 'Your story of Rik & Kara' now introduces continuous writing. The diagrams of the Planets and maps of the world have proved particularly useful in encouraging both hand-eye co-ordinatory skills and the interpretation of visual information. It appears that pupils welcome the opportunity to map and explore their world and to do so in the context of 'reading'.

'Look' gives pupils the chance to make their own typograms. This activity requires that they know what the word means and that imagination is used to embody the meaning in the way it is written. Trials in schools have shown that children will take considerable trouble over this activity and that some reveal wit, imagination and

100

skill in its execution. However, in concentrating upon the visual and calligraphic aspects they may well omit letters—as we all do, if we are not careful, when lettering posters!

The 'About You' sections appear at the beginning and end of this Workbook. Some children become so involved that they want to do them both, one after the other. There is no objection to this, of course, and perhaps it should be emphasised here that there is no need to follow through the books page by page: most children prefer to find an interesting section and do it no matter where it comes in the Workbook. As the involvement of pupils is the be-all-and-end-all of education, the important thing is what they do, not the order in which they do it.

Some pupils may still need help with the instructions which precede the sections and it has been assumed that teachers will explain and give examples to these children so that they know what is expected of them.

The more conversation the books and Workbooks of the Data scheme occasion, the more effective they will be in developing the pupils and their reading and writing abilities. Here it is important to underline the personal nature of the Workbooks: pupils who are encouraged to feel that the Workbooks are theirs, and about them and their activities, will be most inclined to persevere with them and to present their work clearly and accurately. Handwriting and printing, drawings and diagrams will indicate clearly the degree of involvement and the progress made. The reverse is also true: *pupils who are 'left to get on with it' are unlikely to give of their best.* For the involvement of teacher and child, the interaction which is an essential part of education, can only be effective if the teacher is there to explain and encourage, prompt and praise, while the child is actually involved with his work. Retarded readers will not be helped if their Workbooks are decorated with 'iron crosses' after they have completed them: they need help and guidance *when* they are working. In this way we shall achieve what Martin Buber called the 'pedagogical intercourse'.

Data 7—'A Dog for Jerry'

This story and 'Trouble with Bruff' have as their setting a working-class family living on an 'estate', on the edge of an urban area, where town and country interact. It is a situation familiar to many children. Jerry pits his wits against his house-proud mother and garden-proud, crane-driver father to get a boxer dog from the Animal Rescue organisation. The need felt by boys and girls to have their own pets is again a feeling with which they are familiar. Pupils will identify with Jerry, appreciate his relationship with his brother Rod who already has a girl-friend, Jill, and whether or not they have been in slight conflict with their parents over a pet, will certainly have no difficulty in recognising the problem from their own experience. No attempt has been made to produce a stereotype of working-class life or of working-class speech; the situations and conversations are only developed insofar as they contribute to the story and the reader is free to relate what he reads to his own situation without the imposition of generalised assumptions. What is important is Jerry's role as an efficient, likeable, resourceful and successful character in a family situation. From the beginning he shows singleness of purpose and restraint: " *'We've got to get that dog,' Jerry said. It was hot. Rod could splash him as much as he liked.*" Children will see here the germs of a situation in which they have 'lost out' by allowing themselves to be diverted and will appreciate Jerry's tactics. Again, Jerry knows how to make a telephone call, how to care for his dog when he gets it and, at the end of the story, falls asleep while reading how to train his dog. Throughout the story the emphasis is upon Jerry's disposition, his posture, towards his situation as an effective personality. Teachers who have allowed these strands to emerge from discussion have found that their retarded pupils are quick to seize upon this aspect of the story and to relate it to their own family and social situation; they are also well aware of the responsibility of looking after pets and the havoc wrought by neglected dogs.

Conversation is used to carry the story along and is used in short simple sentences. The story falls naturally into six short chapters and, with illustrations on every page, short paragraphs and simple vocabulary, the book encourages children to read with speed and internalise the situations. This process is also fostered by direct reporting of Jerry's thoughts.

Preliminary or follow-up activities may well centre around such subjects as the R.S.P.C.A., dog licences, breeds of dog, pets, pedigrees, and situations in which the interests of parents and children, brothers and sisters, may be at variance. 'Street sharp' children are often able to 'get things done' but lack articulateness. 'A Dog for Jerry' provides starting points for discussions in which conversation, persuasion and communication, are encouraged.

Data 8—'Trouble with Bruff'

This is the sequel to Data 7 but is self-contained and develops both the character of Bruff and of Jerry, who is now brought into conflict with authority in the persons of the irate farmer and his parents. Interest is sustained both by the incidents involving Bruff and Jerry, and Jerry's realisation that, unless he can train his dog, he may have to part with him. The language remains simple but now makes slightly more demands upon the reader's concentration if the adventures are to be followed and fully understood.

Like its predecessor, this book has been designed to look like a substantial reading book. The lines are justified and there are 92 pages to be read. Teachers will appreciate, however, that the large print, 'leading' between lines, wide margins and illustrations at each opening, and simple vocabulary, enable children to read these books quickly and enjoy a consequent feeling of mastery and achievement. If we are concerned to establish the skill and habit of reading we must at the same time establish the habit of reading *books*.

Data 9—The Third Workbook

This Workbook introduces a number of new activities: alphabetic order; classifying words in generic 'sets'; simple codes; surveys of interests, hobbies and pets; and questions which require pupils to consider the consequences of actions—'One Thing Leads to Another', and the reasons why things are made in a particular way—'Why?'. It is doubtful if any children in school, no matter how intelligent, could derive full benefit from all these activities without some help and guidance. Retarded readers and slow-learning children will only benefit if they are given not only help and guidance but adequate opportunity for oral discussion. The reason for their inclusion is to stimulate discussion with their form-mates and teachers and this alone will make their writing both possible and significant. Thus, it is not the completion of the block charts which is important, but the discussion, which will yield the information to be recorded, which is of value to the children.

All these activities, whether it be the correct spelling of their form-mates' names or finding out about keeping tropical fish, should give rise to *speech* in real situations which in turn leads to recording in symbols or words. This places *writing* in a real and significant situation. Once children have recorded their findings they should be encouraged to discuss them and to read them out: this completes the cycle, by placing *reading* what they have written in a real situation.

'Secret Codes' provides an activity, which pupils enjoy, which concentrates attention upon the alphabetic nature of print and its own encoding principles. Like typewriting, codes demand attention to each letter of a word and for this reason are used in subsequent Workbooks as a means of focusing attention upon orthography.

The sections 'Where are You?' and 'Facts to Find Out About Animals' are more searching than similar activities in the earlier Workbooks and involve closer and more extensive reading of information books.

The 'About You' questions now concern themselves with matters of taste, emotions and personal relationships as is appropriate to the growing maturity of the pupils. Again there may be important indicators to teachers of the children's conflicts and uncertainties of identity; discussion will help to clarify and externalise these, perhaps. The final piece of continuous writing, 'Brother Trouble', may also be revealing in this connection.

By the completion of this Stage pupils have met the majority of common consonantal and vowel clusters in both writing and reading,

105

should be reading more widely than the confines of the Data series, will be familiar with the use of books as tools and should now be able to become absorbed in a book. However, they may still be meeting difficulties both with words and with more complex sentences and particular care is needed at this stage in their progress. It is at this level of development in reading skill that interest and motivation must be maintained otherwise children will not progress from the ability to read simple books and the popular press to the stage at which they can learn to learn from books. Moreover, they still need to become aware of the variety of experience to be gained from reading and teachers should continue to read aloud to children from as wide a range of books as possible.

Stage Four   *'Reading Age' 10-11 years*

> Data 10   'Data on Cowboys'
> Data 11   'Dead Man's Trail'
> Data 12   The Fourth Workbook

Data 10—'Data on Cowboys'

From the cinema and television children will be familiar with the mythology of the 'western'. The purpose of this book is to tell them something of the history and geography behind the 'myth'. In common with the majority of adults, children may enjoy 'westerns' but have very little conscious knowledge of the reality; in fact, they often have a fund of latent knowledge which they have acquired but which has not been organised. Thus, they may accept that many 'westerns' revolve around struggles between ranchers and rustlers, between the cowboys of the open range and homesteaders, between cattlemen and sheep farmers, but they are unlikely to be conscious of these classic ingredients or the facts behind them. Interestingly enough, once they do become aware of the reality they will be surprised not by the inaccuracies and anachronisms of TV's 'horse operas' but at the amount of detail they have previously overlooked in them. One group of children who read this book announced the following week that they had seen films in which barbed-wire, remudas, straw bosses and the Chisholm trail were mentioned or depicted; previously they had not 'heard' these words in 'westerns', they had swept over them.

106

Before children begin reading this book teachers may try to encourage them to describe 'westerns' they have enjoyed. If they have not done so before, teachers will be surprised at the difficulty this causes: often only a few confused and unrelated incidents can be described—and yet the children protest their enjoyment and understanding! The action, like the words, has swept over them. We invariably find that our own knowledge and imagination is taxed in our endeavours to give them the words which will give some order and meaning to their experience. 'Data on Cowboys' is an attempt to give the words, the order and structure the children need.

This book condenses in simple language a considerable amount of historically accurate information. It avoids the glib and sweeping generalisations of history text-books, on the one hand, and the romanticised view of the lone cowboy who rides into and out of the scene in so many popular tales, on the other. It concentrates on the detail which children enjoy and which is the proper stuff of history.

There is another dimension to this account which teachers may help to make explicit to their pupils. It is summed-up in the sentence, 'The cowboy showed that men could live in the rolling sea of grass'. The adaptation of man to his environment and man's adaptation of his environment to his needs are both themes which run through the book: the destruction of the buffalo, the vanishing longhorns, the fencing of the open range and the gradual westwards spread of homesteaders and the railroad demonstrate the interaction of man and environment.

The third theme which underlies the narration is that of the qualities of independence and self-reliance, endurance and loyalty which were demanded of the common cowboy. We are not here postulating these characteristics as eternal virtues, that is for the reader to decide; but the fact that they were recognised, at least in retrospect, as characteristics provides a basis for discussion by adolescents about their own standards and values. Whatever ethics or morality cowboys may have possessed, these characteristics were born of their function and their predicament and not imposed by laws. It is not without significance that 'westerns' are inevitably 'moral' despite their trappings of violent action.

Children will need help with the 'particular' words which are used more frequently in this book and some retarded readers will not wish to read it from cover to cover. There is no reason why they should be persuaded to do so. But experience in schools indicates that the illustrations and short topics encourage perseverance and, if teachers are prepared to talk about them and to read some of the more difficult passages, the majority of pupils will want to, and be able to, read the book through. This book is designed to establish 'learning from reading' and marks the beginning of a new level of reading ability. Until now the retarded readers have been learning the skill of decoding print and, whilst this may still be insecure and need attention and a continued gentle gradient of difficulty, are now able to benefit from the exercise of that skill. For this reason a subject which has universal appeal was chosen. The formidable task of reading a straight, factual 'history' has been greatly assisted by Trevor Stubley's brilliant and historically accurate art-work which contributes to the atmosphere and to the visualisation of the text.

Data 11—'Dead Man's Trail'

Retarded readers who have read the previous book will find light relief and little difficulty in reading this 'western'. The action of the story is fast-moving, the situation one which children have no problem in comprehending. Nick Kane and his sister, Jane, are homesteaders whose father has been shot down by cowboys and, therefore, have every reason to be suspicious of the Texan, Ed Fox, whom Nick finds lying on the trail where he's been thrown by his horse. With the help of Eagle Feather, Nick finds the Texan's missing herd of cattle where the rustlers have hidden it. Girls will discern more than boys, perhaps, in the developing relationship between Jane and Ed Fox.

The book is illustrated and designed to look like an authentic 'western' and the mezzotint quality of Richard Young's illustrations help to establish this. But, unlike the old 'penny dreadful' of the past or today's paperback 'western', the book is printed in bold, clear type on thick, white paper in the interests of legibility and easy, fast reading.

This book is unashamedly written to give retarded readers the reward of vicarious experience and a yarn full of action. It is hoped that this has been done successfully despite the absence of blood, bullets and bodies which are dispensed with after the first page.

As was noted earlier, identification with the heroes Nick Kane, Ed Fox and Eagle Feather is provided for boys of all ages, whilst girls will find in Jane a mature and resourceful, as well as attractive, heroine. The situations and characters of this story are both more complex and more mature than those of the earlier books in the series but, apart from the 'particular' words such as 'sheriff's posse' and 'corral', for example, the vocabulary and sentence structures permit easy reading. Teachers should encourage children, therefore, to read this book in as few 'sittings' as possible so that the habit of reading a book through is developed. If this is not done children will find reading stories and novels difficult because of the problem of remembering the significance of what has already been read. This problem should not arise with books which are so profusely illustrated as those in the Data series, as the illustrations serve as reminders, but it may well arise in other books children choose to read.

Data 12—The Fourth Workbook

This Workbook has three sections which involve questions about the facts in 'Data on Cowboys'. Their purpose is both to exercise vocabulary and to provide an opportunity for the children to use the knowledge they have gained. In the process they will also make conscious much of the information lying dormant in their minds and also be made aware of the need for attentive reading. If they have forgotten the facts the instructions suggest that they should look for them in the book: this, too, encourages habits of study. The three sections are 'Which?' and 'Which is Which?', consisting of multiple-choice questions, and 'To Start You Writing'. The first section, 'Cowboy Kit', may also involve the slower children in reference back to the book, but the majority of children will have no difficulty with this introductory exercise.

Two maps, 'Rivers The Cowboys Crossed' and 'The States of The West', involve the use of school atlases and extend the pupil's knowledge of the subject, whilst the sections headed 'Facts to Find Out' and 'More Facts to Find Out' require the use of information books. Geography and history text books may also prove helpful. The

'Facts to Find Out' section draws attention to the fact that there are 'cowboys' in many other parts of the world besides 'the West'; 'More Facts to Find Out' is concerned with the American Indians. The aim of the maps and these two sections is to stimulate wider reading and the relation of what is known to new knowledge. This Workbook, therefore, is largely concerned with involving the retarded reader in the mainstream of education and relating reading ability, which should now be fairly secure, to a wide range of activities in the school curriculum.

There are no 'About You' sections in this Workbook. Instead, 'TV in the Charts' encourages an examination of the popularity of various types of programme and is intended to provide a basis for group discussion. Pupils will be helped if they are given guidance as to how to collect their form-mates' opinions before filling in the charts. The section 'Tough and True' is a substitute for 'About You' as it is designed to elicit the pupils' concepts of a hero, heroine and villain. These two sections should not only give rise to conversation and discussion: they should provide teachers with insights into the interests, opinions, values and standards of the children.

This Workbook contains three opportunities for continuous writing. 'A Cowboy's Log' calls for an imaginative account of a day on the trail, written in the form of a diary; the 'First Meeting' and 'Last Meeting' ask for story-writing concerned with personal relationships, the former between Nick and Eagle Feather, the latter between Ed Fox and Jane. They both appeal to the emotional preoccupations of adolescents and experience suggests that, if discussion precedes writing, the results will be of a high standard.

Stage Five   *'Reading Age' 11-12 years*

Data 13   'The Data Book of "Joe Miller" Jokes'
Data 14   'Once Upon a Space'
Data 15   The Fifth Workbook

Data 13—'The Data Book of "Joe Miller" Jokes'

The purpose of this book is to make the children laugh. It provides on each page a riddle or conundrum, a number of old jokes and a cartoon from 'Punch'. Arthur Koestler's 'The Act of Creation

(*Hutchinson, London, 1964*) opens with four perceptive chapters on humour which should be read by all teachers. As Sir Cyril Burt writes in his Foreword to the book, 'it supplies a fertile set of premisses from which the practical teacher as well as the psychological research-worker can reap a rich harvest of fruitful ideas'.

Humour, according to Koestler, 'is bisociative—perceiving a situation or event in two habitually incompatible associative contexts.' Although this book only presents 'Just a lot of jokes', many of which pupils will have heard before, if it succeeds in making the children laugh, it demonstrates their ability to think about and react to what they have read. Most importantly, it demonstrates to the child his ability to enjoy reading and establishes in his mind that reading is a self-rewarding activity.

Humour relies upon our understanding of words and the situations they create and some of the jokes and many of the cartoons will not immediately evoke laughter or even mild amusement in some children. They may be bad jokes, of course, but we refer here to those which may not be adequately understood. If a few words will quickly establish the situation then children may be helped to 'see' the point, but will not be likely to laugh. Returning to the joke or cartoon later may, however, evoke laughter. For example, the 'howler', 'Napoleon said that England was a nation of shoplifters' assumes that we know that he is supposed to have said 'shopkeepers' and that we understand the meaning of 'shoplifters'; explained in this way the joke is dead but may well cause a smile if we subsequently come upon it unexpectedly.

The cartoons may amuse because of the humour in their execution but they frequently demand both perception of an 'irregularity' in the depiction and an understanding of the total situation presented by cartoon and caption. Children may not immediately realise that the child being returned to his mother from a helicopter has been rescued in the cartoon on p. 20 or know the phrase 'boot licking' which is assumed in the cartoon on p. 12.

These points are mentioned not because we are concerned that teachers should explain the jokes or refrain from explaining them: we wish to draw attention, rather, to the opportunities which exist for discussion and the development of both perception and understanding of situations and language. Whilst we may not contribute to the child's enjoyment of the joke we may well wish to take the opportunity to plug the holes in his knowledge and understanding.

This book gives light relief after the heavy load imposed by the previous Workbook but, nonetheless, provides a unique opportunity for a repetitive vocabulary and the use of words in a wide range of everyday activities. The 'concrete verse' on p. 26 employs a number of echoic words and is evocative of the pain we experience at having to laugh at jokes we have heard before. It may well be used, together with the verses on p. 25, to encourage pupils to write their own comic verse and to make their own collections of verse and limericks.

Telling jokes is a difficult matter. The moment has to be right, the joke appropriate both to the situation and the audience. Children find this difficult to judge or enjoy 'shocking' the teacher. But it is generally accepted that jokes both permit a latitude beyond normal conventions and are most successful when least profound. If the right balance can be established in a Form or group then children can be helped in the telling of jokes and the asking of riddles. Their natural tendency is to take too long in coming to the point and to gabble at the very point at which the denouement is reached. The teacher who has a natural ability to tell jokes well may begin by giving some examples but for the majority of us we would be on safer ground to use a record or tape of a professional comedian. Children will quickly appreciate the timing and the economy of words and will then benefit from opportunities to present their jokes or the jokes from the ' "Joe Miller" Book' and to discuss one another's efforts. Here is an excellent way to encourage good, clear, speech, and to increase fluency and confidence.

Data 14—'Once Upon a Space'

The three short stories in the SF genre are intended to develop reading speed, imaginative visualisation of what has been read and extend the children's familiarity with the registers of reading. The first story is written in the first person, the second is allegorical in both subject and style, whilst the third introduces an internal narrative—although this device was briefly used in 'Dead Man's Trail' for

Ed Fox's account of himself, it is used here to describe all the action concerned with the subject of the title of the story 'The Dead Planet'. It is important to recognise that although adults are so accustomed to these three 'forms' that we scarcely notice them, retarded readers are possibly meeting them for the first time in print.

The use of the first person singular in 'Look-see on Planet Rokh' aids both identification and participation in the story which contains much more descriptive writing than has been used previously. An attempt has been made to create a surreal environment which can only be fully appreciated by visualisation of what is read. Moreover all the senses are involved as, for example, in: *The heat and the noise hit us. An acid stench burnt the backs of our throats. . . . The whole steaming swamp screamed, howled, screeched, hooted and bellowed at us. The swamp was alive with colour and noise. Will-o'-the-wisps shot blue flame through the mist*. This is a long way from Zig and Zag, Rik and Kara or Bruff. The words themselves are no more difficult phonetically but the demands they make are considerably greater.

The story-line, therefore, has been kept very simple and is that of a search for a missing crew-man. The illustrations help the child's imagination but neither tell the story nor give a complete picture.

The facet of this story which may escape some children is that which suddenly emerges in the final paragraph which describes *our own fantastic world*. There are opportunities here which teachers may wish to develop; children may well not agree that our world is fantastic or may wish to suggest further examples of the 'fabulous of the ordinary' in our world. It is hoped that this may lead to a deeper and fuller appreciation of their world by the children. This story prepares the way for the 'In Fact' book.

'Day of the Doom' is an allegory of a ghetto society. Teachers must decide for themselves whether their children are mature enough either to appreciate this or to discuss its implications. The story, however, is intended to be read as a story and the medium is the message.

In the 'Day of the Doom' and 'The Dead Planet' personal relationships and boy-girl relationships are presented in a matter-of-fact way. That Iso Haaf and Milo are 'in love' is less remarkable than that they live beneath the sea; the relationship between Mike Volt and Anna

113

Nova is summed up in the final sentence, 'Together they laughed into space'—which is a very broad view!

The final story, 'The Dead Planet', is a story of piracy, for all its inter-planetary 'business', and teachers familiar with Dutch history will appreciate the significance of the use of the name Pete Hein. The names of all the characters in this book contribute to its internationality and it has been assumed that children who have read this far in the Data scheme will have become fully familiar with the spelling of a wide variety of names and, at least, recognise the foreignness of many of the names used in 'Once Upon a Space'.

The style of this story is more varied than that of any of the previous books or stories, changing with the situation, and much of it is in a conversational style with Pete Hein's story occupying almost half of the narrative. The central action of the story requires children to understand that, on the 'Dead Planet', the rocks were living, intelligent 'things'. If they can appreciate this, and trials in schools indicate that they can, then we have made it possible for them to read with understanding and with imagination about situations remote from their experience.

Teachers will notice that these stories, without, it is hoped, any concessions to poor taste, draw upon the mediated experience children have gained from television. The illustrations by William Ireland are both dramatic and suggest the futuristic nature of the stories. At the same time they sustain interest and contribute to both visualisation and understanding.

Data 15—The Fifth Workbook

The three 'Stranger than Fiction' sections, each consisting of a double-page, relate back to the conclusion of the story 'Look-See on Planet Rokh' in particular and the other stories in 'Once Upon a Space' in general, and look forward to the 'In Fact' book in the final Stage. These sections will demand the use of a large number of books and an encyclopedia. A very useful, compact and up-to-date encylpedia for use in the form-room is Hutchinson's 'New 20th Century Encyclopedia' in one volume, but the children now need access to an encyclopedia with an index and with bibliographies to the important entries so that they may find the books they need. It is hoped that only the least able children will find the few lines in the Workbooks adequate for their responses and that the majority of pupils will be encouraged to treat the questions as open-ended opportunities to pursue subjects that interest them to the limit. It is up to the teacher to foster this pursuit of knowledge when a child's curiosity has been aroused. The Workbook is but a starting point and we have endeavoured to trigger off as great a variety of interests as possible in the hope that each child will find at least a few which have a particular appeal.

The interest in humour stimulated by 'The Data Book of "Joe Miller" Jokes' is encouraged by the section 'Hardbacked Humour' in the hope that children will read some of the authors mentioned. Teachers may well wish to read aloud from some of these authors. The section 'Science Fiction' has a similar purpose. Humorous, imaginative and fantasy writing are encouraged in the sections 'Absent-minded Archie', 'You and Utopia 2500 AD' and 'Once Upon a Space . . .', respectively. Pupils often wish to write at greater length on these topics than space in the Workbook allows, especially if there has been stimulating oral preparation.

The 'About You' section, which is concerned with the pupil's value-judgements and feelings, 'If Wishes were Horses . . .', which stimulates creative thinking, and 'You and Utopia 2500 AD', all provide opportunity for group or Form discussion and debate. The importance of these activities cannot be over-stated.

In the previous Workbook, Data 12, the real significance of car index marks was introduced. In this, the Fifth Workbook, car index marks are used to identify all the counties of Northern Ireland, Scotland, Wales and England. The value of this activity in helping pupils to know their way around their country, to orientate themselves and their locality, especially if they are soon to leave school, is as great as the exercise it gives in reading and writing.

Finally, this Workbook continues to provide reinforcement of vocabulary and continues to familiarise children with the vagaries of our spelling. 'Who is What?' is concerned with common occupations and the Morse Code, introduced in the previous Workbook, is used to give the answers to riddles and conundrums.

Data 16—'In Fact'

The facts in this book extend from the origins of the Earth and of man into the future and into space. The facts are presented in capsule form as information 'bits' complete in themselves yet related to the facts around them so that, once a fact arouses interest, the reader's interest is extended. The book may be read through, fact by fact, column by column and section by section; the reader may start at a section which is of particular interest and, having read it, turn to sections which are related; or the reader may skim the book looking for facts of particular interest. It is doubtful if any child who can read would fail to find some facts of interest and not be tempted to want to go on reading other facts. John Wright's illustrations are designed, together with the lay-out of each opening, to trap the eye without diverting attention from the texts. For this reason most of the illustrations are photomontage images which are pleasing and satisfying in themselves but do not communicate factual information; thus they prompt the mind to seek their significance in the text or give a new dimension to the facts which have been read. The purpose of this book is to arouse and develop interest through reading and to demonstrate to retarded and reluctant readers the fascination and the variety of information which may be gained by reading. At the same time the information 'bits' have been selected to illustrate the infinite variety of our universe, ourselves and the plants and animals with which we share our Planet and are presented in such a way as to encourage a sense of responsibility, of concern and of wonder.

Although this book comes in the final Stage of the Data series, because of the more difficult and extensive vocabulary, it is suggested that children should have an opportunity of reading it at any stage in their reading development. This will not only give them valuable additional reading experience, it will help both them and their teachers to identify and stimulate interest. Reluctant readers in particular will benefit from looking at a book in which facts, which are normally buried in pages of black print, stand out sharply and arouse their curiosity.

Many of the facts are amusing, some astound and others are unexpected. It is hoped that many will prompt further investigation and give rise to questions which readers will feel impelled to answer. Some of the facts included are likely to be challenged or are presented with comments which are provocative: if discussion or argument follow, so much the better. And although every endeavour has been made to check and cross-check the facts there is no doubt that many need qualifying. Discussion and enquiry, which it is hoped the facts will provoke, will enable each reader to make his own interpretations and qualifications.

This book, both in its subject matter and its vocabulary, is intended to ensure that retarded and reluctant readers, through the self-rewarding activity of reading, learn from reading and are brought a step nearer the mainstream of education from which their reading disabilities have divorced them. The vocabulary and the diversity of information in this book are more extensive and make more demands upon the reader than those of a popular newspaper. Pupils who have been helped to read this book, although they still need to exercise and develop the higher skills of reading, can now read with confidence and success. They should know, too, that reading is an activity which is a vital part of living.

The plan of the book is to involve the reader by the relevance of the facts to himself as a human being and as an adolescent. In this way the retarded reader is helped in his quest for identity and made aware of the 'nowness' of reality. This process may well need assistance from the teacher who, through his or her knowledge of the pupil, will be able to see points of relevance and significance to the individual child. Although this book may serve only as a book to be skimmed through by the slow-learning children, for all pupils it should be a book to be talked through. '*What do you think about that? Why do you think that fact is there? Could that happen now? Would you have done that? Is that right? Can you find out anything more about that?*'—The questions of the teacher can spur interests and more

117

thoroughly involve the pupils. '*What does this mean? How do we know that? Do you believe that? Where can I find out more about this? Why isn't there a section on . . . ?*'—The questions of the child will indicate needs which have not been met. The book is but an aid and a beginning. Topics and local studies, research and enquiry, collections of facts and illustrations, visits to museums, galleries and libraries are but a few obvious follow-up activities which should arise from this book.

Data 17—'*Fly Away Paul*'

At one level this book is a fast-moving tale of a chase which begins in the south of England, moves to London and proceeds up the M1 to Westmorland, to end on an island off the coast of Scotland. At another level the story is one of industrial espionage and an attempt to seize world power which is foiled by a brilliant West Indian scientist who involves Paul in his strategy of using cybernetic principles to unmask the master-mind behind the plot. And between these two levels is a third: Paul's growing independence and maturity and his relationship with Helen.

Interest in the story is maintained by the reader's identification with Paul, who tells the story, and by the continuous action and change of scene as he is pursued and eventually takes up the chase himself in search of his father and his captors. The short chapters end in 'cliff-hanging' situations as the plot continuously thickens. Helen, whose involvement in the matter Paul at first resents, plays an important part in the adventures and one of the minor themes in the story is Paul's changing attitude both to her and to Alison.

The changing terrain and landscape, the detailed description of the route, including that through the centre of London and, by helicopter, across northern England and Scotland, will be familiar, in part, to many of the readers and has been deliberately included to add to the enjoyment and sense of participation.

Yet, when all is said and done, the measure of the readers' ability to appreciate the significance of what they have read may be assessed not by their competence in describing the complexities of the plot or the geography of the chase but by their recognition of the significance of a single sentence. At the end of the book Paul looks at Helen and

118

realises that he is glad she had come with him. The book ends: '*Next time I waited for her, I decided, I wouldn't hide in a doorway*'.

That sentence refers back to the opening scene of the book: '*I was waiting in the shelter of a shop door-way. . . . I didn't want anyone to see me waiting for Helen, so I kept well back in the shadows. I don't know why*'. When readers can appreciate the difference between that factual description and the metaphorical reference to it at the end of the book then they will have developed something of the higher skill of reading which is the ability to see meaning behind the meaning of mere words.

The book raises a number of topics quite apart from that of Paul's relations with Helen. There is his attitude to his father, to authority, to Dr. King and to Hogben who is but a pawn in the game like himself. Paul is, like the younger Jerry in the earlier books, a resourceful and independent character, but Paul is a young adult only on the brink of the adult world and yet suddenly thrust into the midst of it in a violent and vital way. This is a situation which is implicitly significant to the adolescent reader but it may need to be made explicit by the teacher.

Paul's attitude to women and society's changing attitudes to them will, like the other topics, also suggest opportunities for discussion and debate. The larger subject 'power', whether in terms of information and its use and control, economics or politics, brought out at the end of the book when Dr. King exclaims '*But not a place for people!*' may well exercise the minds of those pupils who have read and enjoyed the two books in this final Stage.

But, above all else, this is a book to be enjoyed at whatever level it is read or understood. In drawing attention to topics which may give rise to conversation, discussion or debate, our concern is not with the book and its appreciation and understanding by the readers, but with the readers themselves as young adults, as people. If the book has only pleasantly whiled away a few hours it will have succeeded in being 'an entertainment' and if, in books, our retarded and reluctant readers have attained to that then as teachers we have opened the door to the thousands of books which await them. If, by our interaction with them, we may guide their reading and thoughts to more important areas of human endeavour and concern we may do so in the knowledge

119

that now they are secure in the skill of reading and equipped to explore and to begin to appraise literature and their culture. They will have learned to learn through reading, have become imprinted with print and be free to enjoy and to contribute to the mainstream of education.

Data 18—The Sixth Workbook

This, the final Workbook, is designed to project the thoughts of the pupils forward to their futures when they will have left school and to provoke them into talking about and writing about some of the problems of the society into which they are growing. Health, conservation, safety, first-aid, fashions, pollution, jazz, crime, population, famine, marriage and family responsibilities are some of the topics raised. Teachers alone can decide, on the basis of their knowledge of their pupils, what use to make of the opportunities provided for enquiry, research, discussion and debate. Whatever they decide will contribute to the language and intellectual development of the children.

This Workbook also suggests a wide range of facts to be found which will involve wide and perceptive reading. We always learn more if we have a purpose in view but it is also a common experience that what we learn incidentally and perhaps by chance in our pursuit of a subject is of more significance than what we may learn of the subject itself. It may matter little what 'tortillas' or 'carats' are but who can predict what we may discover on the way to finding out? Again, as in the previous Workbooks, our concern is that children shall be learning to use books as tools. It is not a question of knowing the answer so much as knowing how to find it. Teachers may well wish to involve a trained and experienced librarian to advise the pupils in this vital skill.

The maps and international registration letters are used to introduce the countries and many of the physical features of Europe, whilst other sections are designed to encourage an interest in inventions and history. Vocabulary and orthography, sentence, paragraph, narrative, dialogue and imaginative writing are developed and teachers may wish to devise further activities based on the models provided. These may well be combined with follow-up activities initiated by 'In Fact'.

'Finding Facts' probes more deeply than any of the previous

Workbooks into the abilities of pupils to understand and interpret what they have read. A large number of detailed questions are asked about a newspaper report and many children will need help with this. In some instances teachers may wish to provide preliminary exercises using more simple texts. But it is suggested that this activity, which is used in training adults in 'rapid reading', is also valuable in demonstrating to pupils that, with a little concentration and thought, they can learn to absorb a considerable amount of information from an initial reading of a passage which may be recalled when questions are asked about it. However, it is not a skill which can be acquired without practice and concentration. The process may be demonstrated by the teacher reading aloud a short news item and then asking oral questions about it.

Children who find the passage difficult, of course, will benefit simply from reading it and by referring back to it to find each answer. By the time they have answered all the questions they should not only be able to read the passage more easily but have gained reinforcement by writing out their answers. Children who can read the passage with ease, however, may well be encouraged to attempt the answers from memory as suggested above. Having done so they may complete the questions and check those they were able to do by referring to the text.

The Ogam, or Ogham, code introduced in this book, in common with the codes introduced in the previous Workbooks, is used as a device to concentrate attention upon the individual letters of each word, in the same way that 'The Sound's the Same' and 'Printers' Errors' sections draw attention to letter clusters and syllables. In this Workbook 'A Howl of Howlers' involves understanding both of the howler and of the original intention and may, therefore, lead pupils to use dictionaries, to find the meanings of words such as 'vixen', or encyclopedias to discover what the Matterhorn may be. 'Word Ways' is concerned with the origins of words and this is a topic which is well worth developing. It is also suggested that vocabulary may be extended now by introducing pupils to common prefixes such as *anti-*, *bi-*, *con-*, *dis-*, etc., and to suffixes such as *-ancy*, *-ence*, *-ism*, etc. Within the compass of the Data scheme it has only been possible to introduce a few of these (*-ician*, *-ology*, for example) and, it is suggested, that the prefixes in particular are important morphemes which provide clues to the meanings of many common words.

This Workbook, therefore, like its predecessors, should be seen as an opportunity both to extend the interests and language skills of the pupils and to indicate their needs for further help. Activities which the children enjoy doing may well be used to overcome difficulties which inhibit them from attempting other activities. Thus, an interest in codes and ciphers may be used to reinforce spelling or be linked with letter-frequency counts, introduced in 'In Fact', to increase powers of logical reasoning; children who enjoy finding out facts but who still need help with reading may be encouraged to find out information about words, their origins and meanings. The permutations are considerable. At the same time the great variety of activities and devices introduced into the six Workbooks provide teachers with models which may be adapted and modified to meet the specific needs of a particular child at a particular stage in his development. These models, combined with the examples of letter clusters listed in the appendices, give teachers a wealth of resources. Using them to help the individual child at the appropriate time in the most effective way, using strengths to overcome weaknesses, is the essence of the developmental approach we have outlined in this book.

Especially, if it is easy, successful, purposeful—and fun.

APPENDIX A

ONOMATOPOEIC, ECHOIC AND IMITATIVE WORDS

Because the sounds of these words suggest their meaning they are excellent for introducing children to the encoding of words and sounds into print and to many of the common letter clusters. They present little problem of meaning if used in appropriate and, where possible, dramatic contexts. However, we should not delude ourselves into imagining that there is a perfect sound-sense correspondence— the sound 'low' conventionally represents the noise made by oxen but not in France where they drink it.

Children who find difficulty in associating sounds with print will be helped if these words are used to demonstrate the sounds, words, blends or letters with which they are unfamiliar. They will also be useful in demonstrating sounds they may mispronounce or omit. For example, '*hiss*', '*honk*' and '*howl*' may be used to help those who drop the aspirate; '*thump*' and '*thunder*' may encourage the tongue to emerge between the teeth; '*ding*', '*dong*', '*ring*' and '*spring*' will draw attention to the importance of the final 'g' with those who habitually say '*runnin*'' and '*comin*''.

If echoic words can be used in play situations ('*What goes bang?*' or '*How many words can you think of beginning with b as in "Bang!"?*' etc.) aural perception will be encouraged. Children will also enjoy making their own words for sounds and actions. In these activities there are opportunities for language work as the words only have significance in association with actions or things and in situations which have to be described. If we ask 'What splutters? Why did it splutter? How did it splutter?', for instance, children must think, imagine and formulate their responses in words. We may also stimulate children to use these words in stories, rhymes and jingles.

In this connection, it should be borne in mind that many children are not sure of the meanings of many words we commonly use in teaching them to read. In activities with echoic words we may make sure that they do know what we mean when we use words such as '*sound*', '*letter*', '*word*'. We can also introduce '*rhyme*', '*accent*',

123

'*vowel*', '*consonant*', '*blend*' or '*cluster*' and ensure that we have established a working vocabulary to use in our teaching which the children use with certainty and confidence. Once we name a thing we change our attitude towards it, we recognise it and use it to differentiate between other things.

The words are arranged here in alphabetical order but they can be readily selected for their final or vowel sounds. In using them teachers will recognise the importance of children saying the words, using them in appropriate situations and both copying and making writing patterns with them so that they become familiar with them in print. They may also be used as the basis for calligrammes and typograms: executed imaginatively they become sight-sound-symbols which mean what they look like and sound what they are!

ONOMATOPOEIC AND IMITATIVE WORDS

Ah!
Atishoo!

Baa
babble
bang
bawl
bellow
blabbing
blather
blob
blip
blurt
bluster
bobbing
bomb
boo
boom
bound
bray
bump
burble
burst
buzz

Cackle
caw
chatter
cheep
chink
chirp
chortle
chuckle
clang
clank
clash
clatter
click
clink
cluck
cock-a-doodle
coo
cough
crack
crackle
crash
creak
creep
criss-cross
croak
crow
crumple
crunch
cry
cuckoo

Dabble
dap
dash
dawdle
dazzle
diddle
din
ding
dither
dizzy
dodder
doodle
doom
dribble
drizzlc
dump

Echo
Eh!
—er—
erupt
explode

Fee-fie-fo-fum
fiddle-faddle
fizz
flabby
flap
flash
flick
flicker
flip
flit
flop
frizzle
fuss

Gabble
gag
gaggle
gasp
Gee!
ghastly
gibber
giddy
giggle
glitter
gloomy
gobble
gong
grate
grind
grizzle
groan
growl
gruff
grumble
grunt
guffaw
gulp
gurgle
gush
guzzle

Ha!
Ha-ha!
hack
haggle
heave
heckle
hee-haw
He-he!
Hello!
Hi!
higgledy-
piggledy
Hip-hip-
hooray!
hippety-
hoppety
hiss
honk
hoot
howl
hubbub
Hullo!
hullabaloo
hum
humdrum
Humph!

Itchy

Jab
jabber
jammed
jangle
jarring
jeer
jerk
jiggery-pokery
jungle
jink
jittery
jog
jostle
judder
jumble
jump
jut

Knock

Lo!
low
lull
lullaby

Miaow
moan
mumble
munch
murmur
mutter

Nagging
namby-pamby
natter
neigh
nick

O!
Oh!
ooze

Pah!
pat
patter
peep
peewit
Phew!
pitter-patter
plod
plonk
plop
pooh-pooh
pop
prang
prattle
purr

Quack

Racket
rap
rat-a-tat
rattle
ring
rip
ripple
roar
rowdy
rub-a-dub
rumble
rumpus

Scratch
scream
screech
Sh!
shatter
Shoo!
shriek
shrill
sigh
sizzle
slam
slap
slash
slither
slobber
slop
slosh
slush
smack
smash
snarl
sneeze
sniff
snigger
snooze
snort
snuffle
sob
spank
spirt
splash
splutter
spring
sprinkle
spurt
squash

squawk
squeal
squelch
squirm
stamp
swat
swish
swoop

Tapping
tattle
Tehee!
thump
thunder
tick
tiff
ting-a-ling
tinkle
titter
tittle-tattle
toot
tootle
totter
trample
tremble
trill
Tut-tut!
twang
tweet
twiddle
twitter

Ugh!

Waddle
waggle
warble
weep
whack
whang
wheeze
Whew!
whimper
whine
whirr
whirl
whish
whisk
whisper
Whist!
whistle
whizz
whoop
whop
whoosh!
wiggle
wriggle

Yah!
yap
yawn
yell
Yo-ho!
yodel

Zigzag
zing
zip
zizz
zoom

APPENDIX B

PATTERNS OF PRINT

Decoding print assumes a knowledge of the language encoded and of the code. If the directional progression of the code from left to right is assumed, and directionality is fostered in both 'TOLD BY AN ARROW' and 'THE FIRST WORKBOOK', then the process of decoding involves the following skills:

1. a knowledge of letter-sound-sense correspondence as in **I** and **a**;
2. the ability to recognise the letter-sound code's complexity as in the functions of **w** in **'What was Walter writing?'**;
3. the ability to combine sounds in letter clusters such as **'str'** and **'ing'**;
4. the ability to combine the retrieved sounds into words, as in **'string'**;
5. the ability to recognise the approximate nature of the code as in the value of **'a'** in **'Pass the grass path'**, which is subject to regional variation, and as in the values of **'ou'** in **'the boulder country is out of touch . . .'**;
6. the ability to scan, whilst retaining in memory what has been read, before gaining the certainty of sense, as in **'he was bathing the baby'**, **'he was bathing in the sea'**;
7. the ability to learn language from print as in **'The string wound down the hill to the corral . . .'** or **'The pyx is used at the Mint for keeping coins which have to be tested . . . .'**

We have seen that most of these skills are best learned not by decoding print but by encoding language into print. To assist teachers to introduce children to the first five skills listed above we have given in this Appendix examples of the most important aspects of the alphabetic code. Although we have been guided by linguistic and phonetic principles in the selection of the examples and their sequence, we have deliberately avoided over-particularisation. There are three reasons for this: the code is a crude approximation; language is subject to regional and individual variation; we are concerned in reading with sense more than we are with sound. This is immediately apparent when we consider the values of 'th' or the sounds of 'the' in spoken English: although they are constant in print we make the necessary modifications when we read them aloud.

The following sequence has been adopted:

Consonants and short vowels.

Consonants and long vowels.

Consonantal variants: 'soft' C, SC; S in 'sure'; 'soft' G; Silent B, G, H, K, L, N and W.

Consonantal starter clusters: BL, BR, CH, CL, CR, DR, DW, FL, FR, GL, GR, PH, PL, PR, SC, SCR, SCH, SH, SK, SL, SM, SN, SP, SPH, SPL, SPR, ST, STR, SW, TH, THR, TR, TW, WH, QU, SQU.

The Prefix BE—common in many function words and verbs.

Vowel clusters: AI, AY, AU, EA, EI, EY, EE, EO, IE, OA, OE, OI, OU, OY, OO, UE.

Final E and long internal vowel.

Modified vowel sounds: AR, ARE, AIR, ER, EAR, EER; function words with ERE & EIR; IR, OR, ORE, OOR, OAR, OUR, UR, URE, AW, EW, OW, WA, WAR, WOR.

Common final consonantal clusters: CK, CT, CH, TCH, FT, LL, LD, LT, MP, ND, NK, NT, PT, SH, SS, ST, SK, TH.

Mixed vowel and consonant final clusters: ED, IED, ABLE, IBLE, AL, EL, IL, LE, FUL, ING, ANG, ONG, UNG, IC, AGE, DGE, ION, SION, TION, OUGH, IGHT, OUGHT, AUGHT, LY, ILY, NESS, ANCE, ENCE, GUE, OLOGY, ICIAN.

The majority of these clusters are essential for reading the simplest language and are thoroughly exercised in the first two Stages of DATA. Thus the 'soft' **g** is used 20 times in **'giant'** in DATA 2, whilst **'sign'** appears 22 times in the first two books; moreover, the words are used contrastively, **'giant'** with **'great'** and **'sign'** with **'signal'**. Trials in schools have shown that this encourages children to look for the variations of sound and develops confidence to a far greater extent than mere repetition of the same sound or word. Similarly, letter clusters have been used in a variety of words rather than only in the same word. In 'TOLD BY AN ARROW' and 'ZIG & ZAG FROM

PLANET ZV7', for instance, **st** is used 50 times at the start of 15 different words of which 5 start with **str** on 14 occasions; in Stage Two **qu** is introduced and occurs 42 times in 8 different words.

If children experience difficulty with a word it is a simple matter to determine which element in the decoding process has not been mastered. Thus, a child who cannot read **'garage'** in 'A DOG FOR JERRY', in which the word first appears, may be confused because it contains two different uses of **'g'**; reference to the words listed in this Appendix will provide a number of words exhibiting the use of the 'hard **g**', the **ar** and **age** letter strings, which he may be encouraged to write and use in sentences to gain kinaesthetic experience of the pattern.

The word-lists may also be used for the construction of simple diagnostic tests and in activities to supplement those provided in the Workbooks to develop word-attack and spelling skills.[1] For this reason some of the examples given in this Appendix have not been used in the books but have been included to assist teachers to provide additional help where it is needed. A case in point is **'rh'**, which is of very low frequency, and appears in the sixth Stage in **Rhine, Rhône** and **rhyming.** We apologise for having been disinclined to write of either rhubarb or rheumatism!

---

[1] *'Spelling Irregularity and Reading Difficulty in English'*, *by W. R. Lee, Ph.D., N.F.E.R., London, 1957.*

Consonants and short vowels

add	egg	if	off	one	up	hymn
am	end	in	of	once	under	many
an	ever	is	on		until	pyramid
and	every	it	odd		us	busy
as						
at						

bad	can	dad	fat	gag	hat
bed	Celt	den	fed	get	hen
big		did	fit	gift	him
bomb	cod	dot	fog	got	hot
but	cut	dug	fun	gum	hut

jab	kangaroo	lad	man	nap	pat
jet	kettle	let	men	net	pen
Jim	kit	lip	miss	nil	pig
job		lot	mop	not	pot
jug		lump	must	nut	puff

quack	ran	sat	tap	van	wag
quell	red	sell	ten	very	wet
quick	rip	sip	tin	visit	will
	rod	sob	top	volcano	wobble
	run	sun	tug	vulgar	

exam		yap	Zag
expert		yes	zebra
exit			zigzag
export		beyond	
excursion		young	

Consonants and long vowels

April	be	I	go	to	use	Yale	by	apply
able	me, we	ice	no	do	units	yeast	my	reply
age	she, he	like	so	who	duty	yolk	why	nylon
radio	even	sign	over	too	dual	youth	fly	type
				two	you		deny	style

'*Rather father pass the grass after half-past*'—common words with 'a'
subject to regional variations

Consonantal variants

C as in **c**ity **c**entre

city	centre	ice	ace	once	recent
cinema	centimetre	nice	face	since	decent
circle	certain	price	race	voice	December
circus	century	notice	trace	police	receive
cycle	cement	office	place	decide	ceiling
advice	sincere	twice	parcel	choice	reduce

SC as in **sc**ience

science	scene	scent	ascend	scissors	fascinate
scientist	scenery	crescent	descend	muscles	discipline

S as in mea**s**ure & **s**ure

measure	treasure	sure	Asia
leisure	pleasure	sugar	pressure

G as in **g**in**g**er

gem	ginger	age
germ	giant	agent
gentle	giraffe	page
gentleman	gipsy	wage
general	gymnast	stage
generally	danger	message
generous	range	damage
geography	strange	average
geometry	arrange	courage
		garage

131

SILENT **B** as in dumb

dumb	comb	climb
lamb	bomb	tomb
limb	crumb	womb
	thumb	doubt
		debt

SILENT **G** as in gnaw and sign

gnaw	sign	BUT	signal
gnarl	design		signature
gnash	reign		
gnome	foreign		
gnu	campaign		

SILENT **H** as in hour and ghost and Rhine

hour	ghost	Rhine	rhubarb
honest	ghastly	rhyme	rhinoceros
honour	gherkin	rhythm	rheumatism

SILENT **K** as in know

know	knee	knife
known	knelt	knob
knew	knit	knock
knowledge	knight	knuckle

SILENT **L** as in half indicating long vowel

half	talk	yolk	palm
halves	walk	folk	psalm
calf	chalk	calm	almond
calves	stalk	calmly	(salmon)
BUT	could	would	should

SILENT **N** as in hymn

hymn	autumn	column	solemn

SILENT **W** as in write

write	writing	wrist	wreck
wrote	written	wrestle	wrong

Consonantal starter clusters

BL as in **bl**ack

black	bless	blind	blood	blunt
blank	bleed	blink	blot	bluff
blanket	blew	blizzard	block	blush
blast	blaze	blame	blow	blunder

BR as in **br**ing

bring	brake	broke	bread	bright
brick	brain	broad	breath	Britain
bride	brand	bronco	breeze	brother
bridge	branch	brown	break	Bruff

CH as in **ch**urch

chase	chart	check	child	China
chat	chap	cheek	chess	chips
chair	chapter	cheer	children	chop
champion	change	cheese	chest	chuck

CH as in **ch**emist

chemist	ache	school	architect	scheme
chemical	stomach	schooner	orchestra	orchid
Christmas	character	anchor	chorus	choir

CL as in **cl**iff

cliff	clap	clog	clean	clue
click	class	close	clcar	cluster
clinic	clay	cloud	clever	clung
clip	clatter	clock	cloak	clasp

CR as in **cr**y

cry	crab	cross	cricket	crush
cries	crack	across	crisp	crumb
cried	craft	crow	crime	crust
crying	cram	crown	crest	credit

DR as in **dr**op

drop	drag	drive	dry	drama
drip	dragon	driver	drizzle	drum
drown	draw	dream	drift	drank
drink	drawer	dress	drill	drove

DW as in **dw**ell

dwell	dwelt	dwelling	dwarf	dwindle

FL as in **fl**at

flat	fly	flint	flesh	flood
flag	flew	flick	float	flutter
flash	fled	flow	flight	flower

FR as in **fr**om

from	frame	free	friend	fry
frock	fragile	freeze	fried	French
front	frost	froze	Friday	fruit

GL as in **gl**ass

glass	glad	glove	glue	gleam
glitter	glow	glory	glide	gland

GR as in **gr**eat

great	grab	grew	ground	grin
green	grade	grow	gravity	grim
grass	grand	grown	growl	grateful

PH as in **ph**otograph

photograph	pharmacy		'phone	physics
phrase	phew!		telephone	physical
pheasant	Philip		phantom	physician

PL as in **pl**ace

place	plane		plod	plimsolls
please	play		plot	plunder
plan	plate		plug	plastic
plant	platform		plum	plague
planet	plain		pluck	pleasant

PR as in **pr**int

print	prank	proper	promise	proceed
prick	prairie	proud	protest	progress
press	praise	problem	prepare	prompt
prize	price	probably	private	provide
prod	profit	proof	property	programme
prefer	protect	pretend	provide	practical

SC as in score

score	scalp	scatter	Scot	scooter
scar	scale	scarce	Scotland	scoop
scarlet	scare	scarf	scout	sculptor

SCR as in scrap

scrap	screen		scream	scribble
scrape	screech		scrub	script
scratch	screw		scrawl	scripture

SCH as in school

school	scholar		scheme	schooner

SH as in she

she	ship	short	shake	shot
shell	shine	shock	shape	shoot
shelf	shimmer	shone	sharp	shut
shall	shirt	shore	shaft	shrub
shallow	shift	show	shoulder	shrunk

SK as in sky

sky	skin		skimmed	skirt
skies	skid		skate	skull
skip	skill		ski	skeleton

SL as in sleep

sleep	slow	slack	slumber	slit
sleet	slip	slant	slap	slither
slid	slam	slash	slave	slang
slide	slump	sling	sleeve	slice

SM as in small

small	smoke		Smith	smug
smell	smash		smart	smuggle
smile	smack		smooth	smuggler

SN as in snow

snow	snag		snail	snore
snatch	snarl		sneak	sneeze

SP as in space

space	sport	spare	spend	sparrow
speech	spoke	spark	spin	spoil
speak	spoon	spell	spiral	special
speed	spot	spur	spider	spirit

SPH as in **sph**ere

sphere	spherical	sphinx	atmosphere

SPL as in **spl**ash

splash	split	splendid
splatter	splint	splice

SPR as in **spr**ing

spring	sprint	spread
sprang	sprout	sprawl
sprung	spray	sprinkle

ST as in **st**ar

star	stand	stay	state	stomach
start	stair	steam	station	starve
startle	stamp	steal	storm	stage
stop	stampede	stick	story	stone
stockade	stag	still	stork	stump
stocking	stagger	stitch	store	stupid

STR as in **str**eet

street	strip	strain	strict
stretch	stripe	strange	straw
streak	stride	strength	string
stream	strike	straight	strut
stray	stroke	strong	struggle

SW as in **sw**im

swimming	swamp	swallow	sweet	swell
swam	swan	swoop	sweep	swing
swum	swift	swarm	sway	switch

TH as in both **th**is and **th**ing

this	thing	they	then	thirty
that	thin	their	there	thousand
these	think	them	thought	thirsty
those	thick	than	thank	thorn

THR as in **thr**ee

three	throw	through	throb	throne
throb	thrown	throughout	throat	thrust

TR as in **tr**ee

tree	trip	truck	train	treat
travel	tribe	trust	trail	treacle
traffic	trunk	trouble	trade	troop
transport	treasure	trumpet	tremble	true
tramp	try	triangle	trench	truth
	tried	tricycle		
	trial	tripod		

TW as in **tw**ice

twice	twig	twirl	twang	twitch
twelve	twin	twist	tweet	twiddle
twenty	twinkle	twitter	tweed	twilight

WH as in **wh**at

what	whack	whip	BUT	who
when	whale	whirl		whom
why	wheat	whisper		whose
which	wheel	whistle		whole
where	while	white		

QU as in **qu**ick

quick	quiz	queen	quarry	quantity
quite	quote	quest	quarter	quality
quack	quit	question	quarrel	qualify
quake	quiet	quotation	queue	quarantine
		BUT quay		

SQU as in **squ**are

square	squeal	squeeze	squeak	squelch
squadron	squat	squaw	squawk	squid
squirrel		squint		squirt

The prefix BE

became	begin	believe	betray
become	behave	belong	between
because	behead	below	beware
before	behind	beneath	bewilder
began	belief	beside	beyond

Vowel clusters

AI as in **rai**n

rain	gain	aid	tail	nail	wait
train	main	paid	fail	rail	straight
strain	pain	raid	hail	sail	aim
sprain	stain	afraid	mail	trail	brain

BUT 'Certainly said again.'

AY as in **da**y

day	say	tray	pray	holiday	gray
way	may	stray	today	always	sway
away	ray	spray	yesterday	play	pay

BUT 'says'

AU as in **Pau**l

Paul	haul	cause	caught	applaud
Saul	maul	pause	taught	sauce
Claus	haunt	applause	daughter	laundry

BUT 'because'

EA as in **s**ea

sea	ease	eat	peak	reading	leaf
beach	please	meat	speak	leading	leaves
teach	least	seat	repeat	reason	cheap
reach	east	beat	team	season	steal
mean	Easter	heat	steam	beacon	breathe
clean	eager	wheat	stream	dream	peace

EA as in **hea**d

head	ready	meant	tread	breath
read	already	pleasant	spread	death
dead	steady	weather	instead	health
bread	heavy	pleasure	breakfast	wealth
		weapon		

EA as in **great**

great	steak	break

EI as in **ei**ther and/or rec**ei**ve

either	neither	receive	receipt	ceiling

138

EY as in th**ey**

they   grey   prey   obey   convey   conveyor

EY as in mon**ey**

money   monkey   key   donkey   valley   honey   stoney   alley

EE as in s**ee**

see	feet	deed	keep	street	tree	speech
seen	meet	indeed	deep	steep	free	teeth
seem	need	speed	sleep	screen	three	cheer
between	feed	seed	sheep	green	agree	wheel
been	proceed	weed	steel	thirteen	knee	feel

EO as in p**eo**ple

EU as in **Eu**rope

European   Euclid   eucalyptus   neutral   neuter   neuralgia

IE as in t**ie**

tie — tying	try — tries
lie — lying	fly — flies
vie — vying	fry — fries
die — dying	cry — cries, etc.

BUT eye

IE as in p**ie**ce

piece	chief	pier	field	belief
niece	thief	fierce	wield	relief
priest	brief	pierce	yield	relieve
			shield	believe

BUT friend

OA as in r**oa**d

road	boat	coal	moan	oats	toast
load	coat	goal	roam	oak	boast
coach	coast	soap	groan	soak	throat
approach	float	bloater	foal	oath	moat

OE as in t**oe**

toe	goes	Defoe	tomatoes
foe	heroes	Crusoe	potatoes

BUT does and shoe

OI as in p**oi**son

poison	point	oil	toil	coin	noise
voice	joint	boil	toilet	join	moist
choice	rejoice	soil	spoil	avoid	ointment

OU as in **ou**t

out	loud	house	ounce
about	aloud	mouse	pounce
without	cloud	count	found
shout	proud	county	ground
scout	mount	council	pound
south	mountain	announce	round
mouth	fountain	pronounce	sound
BUT	could	would	should
	touch & country		boulder & shoulder

OY as in b**oy**

boy	enjoy	royal
cowboy	annoy	loyal
toy	employ	oyster
joy	destroy	alloy

OO as in g**oo**d

good	took	shook
wood	book	rook
stood	cook	foot
wool	look	soot
	BUT flood & blood	

OO as in s**oo**n

soon	too	cool	food	loop
moon	boot	fool	tooth	swoop
noon	hoot	pool	roof	hoop
spoon	shoot	tool	proof	hoof
balloon	root	room	broom	gloom

UE as in bl**ue**

blue	true	hue	avenue
clue	glue	cue	queue
	rescue		

140

Final E and long internal vowel

hat—hate   her—here   bit—bite   hop—hope   tub—tube
tyre
hop hopping hopped — hope hoping hoped

The 'magic', 'silent' or 'teacher E making the vowel say its name' is, perhaps, the least neglected aspect of reading instruction in schools. Unfortunately, it is often too readily assumed that the children know what 'words', 'sounds' and 'vowels' are or that they are familiar with the sounds of consonants and clusters. High-frequency words such as **some, come, gone, done, have** and **give,** which do not conform to this 'rule', may add to the confusion. The matter is best dealt with, when the need arises, in the context of the children's written work. This applies equally to the plurals of words ending in **y (sky, skies)** and to verbs such as **try** and **reply (tries, tried, trying; replies, replied, replying).**

Spelling, like reading itself, is best taught through writing.

age	these	side	close	tune	type
make	scene	wide	nose	cube	style
name	mere	like	home	salute	rhyme
came	severe	shine	whole	refuse	Clyde
tale	complete	arrive	suppose	excuse	dyke

Modified vowels

AR as in **car**   and **AR** as in simil**ar**

car	arm	chart	similar
card	harm	sharp	regular
mark	alarm	star	circular
dark	hard	far	triangular
garden	Mars	yard	calendar
target	part	charm	standard

ARE as in **care**

care	stare	fare	rare	share	spare
careful	glare	flare	beware	declare	square

AIR as in **air**

air	fair	repair
hair	chair	affair
pair	stairs	prairie

ER as in h**er** and work**er**

her	perhaps	rather	summer	jumper
father	person	other	winter	driver
kerb	perform	never	dinner	shoulder

EAR as in **ear**

ear	rear	clear	appear
hear	fear	spear	disappear
dear	near	tears	beard

EAR as in b**ear**

bear	wear	swear	tear up	pear tree

EAR as in **ear**th

earth	early	earn	heard
earthquake	earl	learn	pearl

EER as in b**eer**

beer	cheer	steer	peer
deer	jeer	sheer	queer

FUNCTION WORDS with **ERE**

here   where   there   nowhere   somewhere   therefore   anywhere

FUNCTION WORDS WITH **EY—EIR**

they   their   theirs

IR as in f**ir**st

fir	sir	bird	third	shirt
first	stir	birth	thirsty	skirt
firm	girder	girl	thirty	dirty

OR as in **nor**th and in mot**or**

north	morning	port	motor	actor
nor	normal	storm	senior	factory
born	orbit	short	interior	history
forget	order	story	exterior	victory
fortune	horse	force	mirror	Equator

142

ORE as in m**ore**

more	shore	wore
store	explore	tore
snore	swore	forehead

OOR as in d**oor** & as in p**oor**

door	indoors	floor	poor	moor

OAR as in **oar**

oar	board	hoarse
roar	hoard	coarse
soar	uproar	hoarding

OUR as in **our**

our	our	sour
hour	ourselves	flour

OUR as in f**our** & in col**our**

four	your	colour	labour
pour	yourself	favour	harbour
course	rumour	flavour	neighbour
court	humour	glamour	behaviour
mourn	odour	armour	endeavour

BUT tour & courage

UR as in t**ur**n

turn	fur	church	purple
burn	further	purchase	curse
furniture	murmur	spur	nurse
curtain	burglar	purse	burst
hurl	hurt	turf	purpose
curve	burden	surface	surgeon

URE as in p**ure** & f**ury**

pure	fury	Muriel
cure	furious	bureau
curious	mural	lure
curiosity	purify	allure

URE as in nat**ure**

nature	picture	future	adventure
capture	mixture	fracture	temperature
feature	creature	posture	departure

143

AW as in saw

saw	claw	jaw	draw	hawk
raw	flaw	paw	drawn	shawl
thaw	crawl	straw	trawler	yawn

EW as in new

new	flew	knew	blew	jewel
few	grew	crew	view	newt
yew	drew	brew	chew	stew

BUT sew

OW as in how

how	now	brown	cow
howl	clown	town	coward
towel	frown	drown	crowd
fowl	crown	power	flower
brow	down	powder	tower

OW as in arrow

arrow	low	owe	know	shadow
bow	slow	own	known	yellow
narrow	show	snow	flown	fellow
sparrow	follow	shown	grown	shallow
pillow	hollow	blow	blown	tomorrow

WA as in want & war

want	wash	wanted	war	reward
wander	washer	wanting	warble	forwards
watch	washing	warrant	warm	backwards

BUT water

WOR as in word

word	work	worth	worm
world	worse	worship	worst

Common final consonantal clusters

.. CK as in ba**ck**

back	neck	lick	lock	luck
black	wreck	brick	sock	suck
clock	deck	trick	rock	truck
knock	speck	thick	shock	stuck
block	peck	stick	frock	buck

.. CT as in fa**ct**

act	attract	expect	collect	direct	conduct
fact	contract	affect	protect	erect	instruct
tact	intact	effect	inspect	neglect	product
pact	inflict	strict	district	inflict	obstruct

.. CH as in mu**ch**

much	which	arch	church	ranch	reach
such	inch	march	crunch	branch	beach
each	pinch	parch	punch	touch	speech
rich	flinch	starch	lunch	crouch	teach

.. TCH as in wa**tch**

watch	itch	fetch	switch
catch	ditch	stretch	clutch
match	stitch	scratch	Dutch

.. FT as in le**ft**

left	soft	raft	swift	shaft
lift	aloft	craft	drift	gift

.. LL as in ba**ll**, be**ll**, bi**ll** & bu**ll**

ball	bell	bill	bull	BUT roll
tall	tell	till	pull	toll
wall	well	will	full	stroll
fall	fell	fill		scroll
small	spell	thrill		
call	smell	skill	BUT Shall	& doll

.. ULL as in d**ull**

dull	lull	skull
gull	seagull	Hull

.. LD as in old

old	hold	held	wild	field
told	bold	weld	child	build
gold	cold	world	mild	shield

.. LT as in halt

halt	melt	bolt	built
salt	belt	colt	fault
felt	Celt	jolt	spilt

.. MP as in jump

jump	lamp	imp	pump
bump	camp	limp	ramp
lump	stamp	romp	stump

.. ND as in and

hand	brand	end	kind	pond	round
land	grand	bend	mind	fond	ground
sand	stand	spend	find	second	found
band	strand	attend	behind	blond	sound

.. NK as in thank

thank	ink	sink	drink	bunk
think	pink	sank	drank	trunk
plank	wink	sunk	drunk	shrunk

.. NT as in want

want	hint	bent	plant	invent
went	print	dent	giant	absent
sent	flint	tent	blunt	present

.. PT as in kept

kept	wept	leapt
slept	accept	erupt
crept	adopt	interrupt

.. SH as in ash

ash	rash	dish	Scottish	blush	polish
lash	crash	Welsh	push	thrush	vanish
splash	Irish	flesh	brush	mash	astonish
clash	fish	fresh	crush	punish	
cash	wish	wash	British	finish	

146

.. **SS** as in dre**ss**

dress	less	miss	toss	fuss
press	mess	kiss	boss	truss
cross	across	pass	grass	glass

.. **ST** as in fa**st**

fast	list	best	west	longest	darkest
past	mist	rest	east	tallest	lightest
last	fist	test	lost	biggest	strongest
mast	first	forest	just	shortest	smallest

.. **SK** as in a**sk**

| ask | mask | risk | dusk |
| task | desk | brisk | tusk |

.. **TH** as in wi**th**

with	north	bath	teeth	length	forth
both	south	mouth	tooth	strength	fifth
bath	death	health	wealth	growth	eighth

Mixed vowel and consonant final clusters

.. **ED** as in talk**ed** & answer**ed**

talked	looked	washed	liked	helped	& answered
walked	jumped	dressed	wished	pushed	opened
stopped					called
					moved
					pulled

.. **ED** as in end**ed**

| ended | traded | started | parted |
| wanted | raided | halted | pretended |

.. **IED** as in tr**ied** & hurr**ied**

| tried | lied | dried | replied | & | hurried | emptied |
| cried | tied | fried | supplied | | worried | buried |

.. **ABLE** as in valu**able**

| valuable | comfortable | probable | miserable | portable |
| washable | remarkable | suitable | laughable | lovable |

.. **IBLE** as in horr**ible**

| horrible | terrible | possible | visible |
| sensible | edible | impossible | invisible |

147

. . AL as in di**al**

dial	special	final	mental	medal	capital
trial	usual	total	dental	metal	royal
dual	casual	animal	normal	canal	vertical
equal	official	hospital	artificial	sandal	horizontal

. . EL as in cam**el**

camel	tunnel	kennel	label	marvel	level
panel	funnel	vessel	navel	mongrel	parallel
model	gravel	towel	novel	travel	vowel

. . IL as in pup**il**

pupil	evil	April	Brazil	pencil
until	devil	Avril	tonsil	daffodil

. . LE as in litt**le**

little	people	puzzle	ankle	example	stumble
bottle	cattle	middle	uncle	simple	grumble
settle	jungle	couple	bicycle	struggle	whistle
apple	jingle	angle	paddle	trouble	needle

. . FUL as in care**ful**

careful	handful	wonderful	thoughtful	awful
helpful	spoonful	beautiful	faithful	painful
carefully	cupful	grateful	faithfully	
			thoughtfully	

. . ING as in k**ing** & runn**ing**

king	string	nothing	running	blowing	making
ring	spring	something	sitting	showing	taking
sing	evening	anything	getting	working	hiding
wing	morning	everything	swimming	bathing	living

. . ANG as in b**ang**

bang	sang	mustang
rang	hang	gang

. . ONG as in s**ong**

song	wrong	along
long	strong	belong

. . UNG as in h**ung**

hung	lung	rung	swung
sung	flung	sprung	strung

. . IC as in traff**ic**

| traffic | clinic | panic | terrific | Atlantic | atomic |
| picnic | comic | frolic | fantastic | Pacific | Arctic |

. . AGE as in **age** and mess**age**

age	rage	message	village	sausage	average	postage
page	wage	passage	cottage	manage	savage	package
cage	stage	language	cabbage	damage	bandage	advantage

. . DGE as in le**dge**

edge	badge	lodge	ridge	cartridge
ledge	wedge	dodge	bridge	partridge
hedge	pledge	judge	grudge	knowledge

. . ION as in fash**ion**

| fashion | union | opinion | religion | companion |
| million | onion | suspicion | region | champion |

. . SION as in televi**sion**

television	tension	decision	admission	mission
vision	pension	occasion	permission	passion
revision	profession	provision	impression	discussion
division	expression	collision	explosion	conclusion

. . TION as in sta**tion**

station	fraction	imagination	collection	precaution
nation	addition	composition	action	caution
direction	subtraction	description	fiction	motion
portion	multiplication	alteration	suggestion	formation
relation	correction	invention	question	information

. . OUGH as in r**ough**

| rough | tough | enough |

. . OUGH as in th**ough** and pl**ough**

| though | although | plough | bough | sough |
| | | BUT through | | |

. . IGHT as in n**ight** & in e**ight**

night	fight	delight	height	eight
sight	flight	slight	knight	freight
light	fright	tight	tonight	straight
might	bright	right	midnight	weight

149

. . OUGHT as in th**ought**

thought	brought	fought	nought
bought	sought	ought	BUT drought

. . AUGHT as in t**aught**

taught	naughty	daughter
caught	haughty	slaughter BUT laughter

. . LY as in dai**ly**

daily	holly	badly	suddenly
silly	holy	gladly	exactly
belly	bully	finally	possibly
jelly	ugly	quietly	quickly

. . ILY as in happ**ily**

happily	merrily	busily	lazily	funnily
luckily	prettily	greedily	crazily	hastily

. . NESS as in good**ness**

goodness	happiness	business	emptiness
darkness	quietness	sickness	gladness

. . ANCE as in dist**ance**

distance	attendance	performance	clearance	finance
entrance	admittance	assistance	chance	dance
advance	ignorance	insurance	glance	instance

. . ENCE as in f**ence**

fence	licence	hence	absence	science
defence	sentence	pence	presence	conscience
offence	commence	essence	residence	patience
intelligence	difference	influence	confidence	experience

. . GUE as in fati**gue**

fatigue	rogue	plague	prologue	brogue
league	vogue	vague	dialogue	fugue

. . OLOGY as in zo**ology**

zoology	geology	meteorology	biology	apology
archaeology				ornithology

. . ICIAN as in mus**ician**

musician	physician	politician	magician
optician	electrician	mathematician	dietician

APPENDIX C

PATTERNS OF WRITING

Sequence of linguistic and phonetic structures developed in the Workbooks

Throughout the Series, the WORKBOOKS highlight specific aspects of language and of the encoding-decoding of language. The exercises provided are intended both as useful activities in themselves and, more importantly, as models on which teachers may base activities specifically designed to assist the individual child. For this reason we have included activities which have been found helpful but which are not commonly used in schools and have avoided those which may discourage further reading such as 'comprehension exercises' based upon what the child has read in the Books.

We have already referred to the importance of the sections headed 'About You' and to those which encourage wider reading and the use of books. Here we are concerned with the sequence of the activities which directly contribute to language and reading-writing skills. However, trials of the Series in schools have shown that, as was anticipated, both the 'Car Number Games' and the map-making activities, are both valuable and susceptible to considerable extension. Any activities which make children conscious of sounds, language and their everyday world greatly accelerate the acquisition of the various skills and are regarded by the children as both purposeful and fun. Combining sounds, say a given vowel with any consonant or cluster, to make words, rhymes, alliterations and assonance, are activities which have developed out of the 'Car Number Games' and other exercises in the WORKBOOKS.

Map-making has been found to be remarkably popular and has revealed both surprising knowledge and surprising ignorance in retarded children: both are invaluable pointers for teachers. Map-making has arisen both from the WORKBOOKS and from the books themselves, in particular, from 'ZAG THE GREAT & ZIG THE BIG', 'DATA ON COWBOYS' and 'IN FACT'. Hand-eye co-ordinatory work which might, at first sight, have been thought beyond many children, when identifying places on one map and transferring recognition of their position to an outline map of a different scale or projection, or from a globe, has been tackled with enthusiasm. Moreover, children have been anxious to go on looking for and entering other places and physical features once they started. The value of this activity, kinaesthetically and cognitively, cannot be overestimated. In many instances it has appeared as if, for the first time, children were busily recording all that they knew about their world and anxious to identify every place of which they had heard. The demands of map-making for clear, neat printing and minute attention to detail when copying the spelling of place-names have also been found to be important contributing factors in this purposeful activity.

Listed in this Appendix are the phonetic and linguistic structures exercised in each Workbook. By referring back to the word-lists in Appendix B teachers may select further examples of the various words, clusters and sounds exercised; by relating the Workbooks to their associated reading books they may identify the books in which the structures are given particular attention.

The Workbooks have been designed to provide teachers with a ready means of identifying children's reading and understanding problems as well as of assessing their ability to write, spell and express themselves. This is their diagnostic function. However, they also provide a useful guide to the vocabulary and reading difficulty of the books which precede them: seen in this light they may be used by teachers to prepare children for some of the language and decoding problems they will meet in the reading books.

> **In all the Workbooks the vocabulary exercised is that used in the previous reading books of the DATA series.**

THE FIRST WORKBOOK — DATA 3

Function words (*here, now, over, through etc.*):	pp. 3, 4, 5, 6, 7, 8, 9.
All single consonant sounds and short vowel sounds:	Car Number Game, pp. 10 & 11.
RIGHT and WRONG and reading for meaning:	p. 14.
High survival value words:	pp. 15, 24 & 25.
Changing sentence structure:	pp. 16 & 17.
'Speech' words (*said, asked, replied, etc.*):	pp. 18 & 19.
BECAUSE and changing sentence structure:	pp. 20 & 21.
Sentence completion:	p. 22.
Sentence formation from given words:	pp. 23, 28, 29.
WHO and sentence writing:	p. 30.

THE SECOND WORKBOOK — DATA 6

Function words and WHO, WHAT, WHICH, HOW questions:	pp. 3, 11, 12, 16, 17, 21 & 23.
Word recognition and classification into 'sets' (e.g. *car & bus: flame & fire etc.*):	p. 5.
Short vowel sounds in Car Number Game:	p. 6.
Writing words for 'set' of ball games:	p. 11.
Correcting word sequence of sentences and identifying clusters—ONE, . . ET, . . OO, . . CH, . . DDLE, . . OR, . . ARE, . . RY, . . UE, . . MP:	p. 13.
Identifying, in words, the clusters—OUND, . . EAR, . . ASH, . . OO, . . IGHT, . . ONG, . . ACK, . . OW, . . EW, . . IDE:	p. 21.
Word-making from letters of a given word:	p. 22.
Writing words for 'sets' of dogs, birds, cars, boats:	p. 26.
Sentence completion:	p. 27.
Function words and WHERE, WHICH, WHEN, WHAT questions:	p. 30.

THE THIRD WORKBOOK DATA 9

Function words with IF, DO, WHAT, WHEN,
  WHICH, WHY questions: pp. 3, 8, 13, 15,
  19, 25, 27, 28,
  29.

Classifying words in 'sets' of food, clothes and
  furniture: p. 4.
Naming the parts of bicycle, face and body: pp. 5, 11.
Changing sentence structure for sense by identifying
  words of similar appearance containing .. ET,
  .. CT, .. EY, .. Y, .. OUND, .. IZE, .. ISE,
  .. DGE, GUA.., GA.., CH.., .. ASHED,
  W.., WR.., .. ETS, .. IE.., .. EA.., K..,
  KN.., .. EAR..: pp. 6, 7.
'Speech' words (*agreed, demanded, explained, etc.*) p. 10.
Alphabetical order introduced: pp. 12, 13.
Identifying in words the clusters—..AY, ..UE, ..EE..,
  final E, ..ECT, ..IE.., ..AI.., ..ET and QU..: p. 14.
Sentence completion: p. 16.
Forming words from consonantal frame in Car
  Number Game requiring use of vowels: p. 17.
Sentence formation from given words: p. 20.
Question formation from given situation: p. 21.
Alphabetic code exercising vocabulary: pp. 22, 23.
Continuous writing introduced: pp. 24, 30.
Classifying pets in 'sets' and making and reading a
  block chart: pp. 26, 27.
'*If you were* ..' questions to be answered: p. 28.

THE FOURTH WORKBOOK   **DATA 12**

APPENDIX D

TYPEFACES AND SIZES USED IN EACH BOOK OF THE DATA SCHEME

DATA 1	'Told by an Arrow'	14 pt. Imprint
DATA 2	'Zig & Zag from Planet ZV7'	14 pt. Imprint.
DATA 4	'Rik & Kara'	14 pt. Imprint.
DATA 5	'Zag the Great & Zig the Big'	14 pt. Imprint.
DATA 7	'A Dog for Jerry'	12 pt. Plantin.
DATA 8	'Trouble with Bruff'	12 pt. Plantin.
DATA 10	'Data on Cowboys'	12/14 pt. Rockwell.
DATA 11	'Dead Man's Trail'	12/14 pt. Bodoni.
DATA 13	'The Data Book of "Joe Miller" Jokes'	12/13 pt. Gill Sans 262.
DATA 14	'Once upon a Space'	13/14 pt. Bembo.
DATA 16	'In Fact'	12 pt. Gill Sans.
DATA 17	'Fly away Paul'	12/13 pt. Baskerville.
DATA WORKBOOKS		13 pt. Grotesque 215.

Index of References to Data Books

Index of Authors

Data on Reading

*The teacher's handbook to
the Data scheme for reluctant
and retarded readers*

PETER YOUNG

SCHOFIELD & SIMS LTD.
HUDDERSFIELD

0 7217 0034 9

First printed 1970

Printed in England by
Henry Garnett and Co., Rotherham and London.